* POLITICS AND THE EARLY CHRISTIAN

Politics *and* *the early christian*

BY

FRANCIS XAVIER MURPHY, C. SS. R.

FOREWORD BY HUBERT H. HUMPHREY
Vice President of the United States of America

DESCLÉE COMPANY, INC.
New York - Tournai - Paris - Rome

TO

EDGAR AND PHOEBE BERMAN

CONTENTS

FOREWORD

by Hubert H. Humphrey,
Vice President of the United States of America

This book by my friend, Father Francis Xavier Murphy, gives a keen insight into an essential element in politics that is also reflected in the pursuit of the Christian ideal: the deep sense of order that must pervade society, through the use of faith and responsibility, to achieve the ideals of social justice and peace.

Father Murphy reveals in historical terms how the state and soul naturally develop in concert because both affirm not only life, but a just life.

In prerequisites, both the soul and the just state demand high motives of man, necessitating sacrifice for a common good; both require the sublimation of man's baser instincts, one for personal serenity and the other for his broader, interpersonal and social relationships. They both make progress through the proper use of intelligence and education; but they can also flourish with only an instinctual feeling for charity and justice.

The historical sequence of man's ideas in the development of both Christianity and the state reveals, even in these early years, the dynamics of change in approach anchored on an immutable centrality of basic themes or principles. This history thus emphasizes the truth that no rigid theories or philosophies can explain or change man; but that the way to his goals is by a meld of the laws of nature and the laws of life; that human nature must be tempered to attain the best of human behavior.

Even in the short period encompassed in Father Murphy's treatise, from the time of Christ to Augustine, there is the glimmer of hope that if Christianity could lead the majority of mankind to personal tranquility, it would go far also towards simplifying the basic problem of political order. Conversely, a free and more orderly politics has done much to allow individual man peace and security to seek higher spiritual fulfillment. It is a complimentary cycle in which both religion and politics present a plan for man—one divine, the other human—with both having their foundations in justice through faith and through the law.

The historical perspective one absorbs in this book gives the feeling that, though modern church and state are separated in our present democracies, the balance is maintained on a sensitive scale of principle, responsibility and function. I think that Father Murphy's own words best epitomize the conviction one comes away with after reading this book:

> Politics, the most worldly of human endeavors, is
> instinct with theological overtones. It is obviously
> concerned with the ordering of the secular city in
> pursuit of justice. But human experience thus far
> indicated that this is impossible unless those dedicated to
> its pursuit are motivated by higher ideals. In search for
> such ideals, man must take into consideration his final
> destiny—and this is beyond politics.

Introduction

*" Seek first the kindgom of God and his justice,
and all these things will be given to you besides "*
(Mt 6,33; Lk 12,31).

While these words of Christ possess a meaning much deeper than their obvious significance in the hellenistic philosophy, they could still be accepted by both greeks and romans as expressing a fundamental principle of political science. For from Homer to Cicero and beyond, the idea of a city or state *(polis)* was an entity founded on justice. It was actually the christian political pessimist, St. Augustine, who quarreled with the principle that he considered rather a pretension than a fact when he asked: "But what are kingdoms if not robber states?" It is not that Augustine did not believe in justice; but that he saw the human attempt to achieve this virtue in political situations constantly undermined by the effects of original sin; and in his attempt to ward off the pagan attacks on the christian way of life he decided to face the issue of political science with total honesty.

One result of this augustinian evaluation of practical political achievement still bedevils christian thinking on the subject. High-minded young men frequently hesitate to enter the arena of politics on the score that this medium of human endeavor is by its very nature evil infested. What they are confusing with politics itself is, however, the vulgarity that often accompanies political campaigns and maneuvers, and the whole art of bribery and intimidation which are considered essential to political rule.

In actual fact, Aristotle designated politics as the highest of human endeavors since it was devoted to the disposition of man's terrestrial life. Though modern usage distinguishes between the role of the statesman and that of the politician, the distinction is more nominal than qualitative. The statesman is presumed to achieve his purposes on a higher plane by a more or less unemotional use of intelligence in pursuing the art of the possible in human affairs, while the politician operates on a level in which instinct and emotion predominate. In actual fact, the technique behind each level of political endeavor, though perhaps differing in immediate application, is basically identical: it is founded on the art of persuasion, which can of course degenerate into oppression; but then it loses the character of politics and becomes tyranny. Political persuasion, on the other hand, has as its objective convincing men to act and live together in peace and harmony.

What vitiates politics and statesmanship is an evil purpose to which the fine art of persuasion may be perverted. Change the objective of political endeavor to domination, even without the use of force or violence, whether for racist, nationalistic, or ideological reasons, or for the bare exercise of wealth or power, and the augustinian perspective of empires or even republics as robber states immediately comes to the fore. A whole millenium before Augustine, Hesiod had come to a similar conclusion in his analysis of just and unjust city-states. Yet men of good will, and particularly those devoted to a christian view of life and the universe, have not the right to abandon political endeavor merely because its circumstances are generally infected with the "evils that men do in this life"; no more than they are justified in abandoning life itself because of the obvious effects of original sin.

Despite the fact that biblical scholars and modern theologians are far from agreement on the exact meaning of the *logion* of Christ, "Seek therefore first the kingdom of God and his justice, and all these things will be added to you besides," that was enunciated in the midst of the Sermon on the Mount (Mt 5—7), the sentence can serve as a proper introduction to a consideration of the political thought of the early christians.

It deals with two basic ideas that constitute the hard core of ancient political speculation among both greeks and romans, and that affected the life and thought of the early church. Whatever may be the technical exegesis of the *regnum Dei (basileia tou theou)* it is obvious that it did not represent a secular state in Christ's use of the term; it is likewise evident that God's justice, to which he calls such immediate attention, far transcends the relationship of spiritual and secular reciprocity embodied in the aphorism *"suum cuique tribue"*—give to every man his due—that is commented upon by St. Paul (Rom 13,7-8), as well as the virtue of honesty that is involved in the worldly ideal of justice.

Christ's reference to justice was aimed likewise at a concern for everyday life, as the context of the quotation clearly proves; and while his frequent descriptions of the kingdom of heaven have an other-worldly localization in the ideals he set before his hearers, the immediate terms in which he expressed himself reflect the political atmosphere of Palestine in the days of Tiberius Caesar. While Christ never mentioned the roman empire to which he as a jew lived in subjection, he was not unaware of its hegemony, and he did speak of men from the east and the west coming to join the children of Abraham in God's kingdom (Mt 8,11).

Along with the authority of the local temple rulers, Christ accepted the secular order into which he had been born; and though in the end he acknowledged that he was a king, he quickly added, "My kingdom is not of this world" (Jn 18,36). This seeming ambivalence in Christ's political adhesion did not present any great problem for the early church; nor does it seem to have disturbed the writers of the New Testament who quite evidently interpreted his deeds and sayings in a uniquely theological sense.

For the modern political philosopher, however, there are numerous difficulties in comprehending Christ's attitude vis-à-vis the state, and his concept of worldly justice, not to mention an understanding of the early christians in their dealings with the circumstances of their contemporary political life. These modern difficulties arise mainly from the attempt to separate

politics from theology, an idea inconceivable to the mind of
ancient man, whether jew or greek or barbarian, for whom
"all things are full of gods." The relationship between theology
and politics as two mutually intertwined categories of human
knowledge and endeavor is beginning to be accepted once
more by the most sophisticated of modern statesmen. [1] For
there is a religious element even in the most determinedly
atheistic state, just as there is a spiritual *élan* generated in
nationalistic and other ideological grasping for territorial or
world hegemony. And the only political psychology capable
of dealing with such pseudo-idealistic drives toward the
revolutionary manifestations of power is one based upon a
theological foundation.

In this respect the New Testament pericopes describing
the temptations of Christ, and of a certainty, St. Paul's observations regarding the "principalities and powers... the world
rulers of this darkness," and the "spiritual hosts of wickedness
in the heavenly places" (Eph 6,12), have something to say to
the modern statesman or political observer.

Political philosophy has a long history, of course, that in
its formal sense, at least, goes back to archaic Greece and is
reflected in Homer, the educator. Among the more influential
of the primitive political philosophers were Hesiod, who commented on the life of the peasants and townsmen in his *Works
and Days;* Tyrtaeus, who stressed virtue *(areté)* as the vocation
of the spartan citizen; Pindar, the voice of aristocracy in
Athens; Solon, the creator of athenian political culture; the
sophists, whose educational and political humanitarianism
requires some attention; Thucydides, the first truly political
philosopher; Plato and Aristotle with their specific attempts
in, respectively, the *Republic* and the *Laws*, and in the *Nicho-
machean Ethics* and *Politics*, to examine human nature and

---

[1] Cf. A. Toynbee, *An Historian's Approach to Religion* (New York, 1956)
244, where, ignoring the thought of Aristotle, he maintains that one of the
few freedoms the monolithic state of the future will allow, will be in the
matter of religion. But this is the first department that such a state must
control. Religion is the one certain source and stimulant of rebellion
against injustice and tyranny.

human behavior in society, as they describe both a practical and an ideal type of state. Finally there is the theology as well as the theory of despotism, or the rule of the tyrants, and the whole gambit of oriental kingship that play a substantial role in the reaction of the early christians to the political milieu in which they found themselves. Most of these ideas and movements can only be mentioned briefly; they are, however, the subject of a vast modern literature, the main achievements of which will be summarily touched upon in the course of this study.

It is with the hope of providing an introduction to this realm of human experience as it was conceived by the leaders of the early church that the present work has been written. Special recognition is due to colleagues and friends who encouraged me in the pursuit of this project, and my gratitude goes in particular to Fathers John Duffy, C. SS. R., and Paul Bryant, C. SS. R., who read proofs and helped prepare the Index. I am, of course, dependent on the scholars who have recently dealt with these tropics, and have tried to give them condign credit in the notes. The ideas at least are part of a series of lectures on the political thought of the Early Church Fathers delivered at the Academia Alfonsiana in Rome in the academic year 1966.

I

The Hellenistic Experience

A formal concern with man's political interests, in essence at least, may be traced to archaic Greece, and to the thunderings of the early hebrew prophets. But the art of politics only truly began with the establishment of the *politeia* in the city-state or *polis*, such as can be seen in the political poetry of Solon. Previous attempts at understanding human dynastic and tribal relationships were lost sight of in the complexity of a group's primitive religious concepts. Most modern anthropologists agree that, from the first awakenings of primitive culture, men had made an attempt to understand the laws of life. They had tried to regulate their family or tribal ways of doing things by their experiences with the forces of nature, no matter in how crude or symbolic a form they may have conceived these powers. [1]

Primitive man saw the earth and sky as a living world of mysterious forces. Its demands had to be observed and satisfied by some sort of ritual, whether religious or magic. Man felt himself as part of the world process; and he had to

---

[1] The bibliography on this subject is extensive. A good introduction is supplied by W. Jaeger, *Humanistische Reden und Vorträge* (Berlin, 1937) and more generally in his three volumes of *Paideia : the Ideals of Greek Culture* (New York, 1934-1944). See also C. Dawson, *Progress and Religion* (New York, 1938); C. N. Cochrane, *Christianity and Classical Culture* (New York, 1944); A. A. T. Ehrhardt, *Politische Metaphysik von Solon bis Augustin*, I and II (Tübingen, 1959); E. Barker, *Alexander to Constantine* (Oxford, 1959).

act in harmony with the divine cosmic powers. Hence the tribal leader or the king was not so much the man who organized or ruled a political community; he was rather the religious head of his people. As such, he served as the representative of the god by his interpretation of the divine desires. Occasionally, he even felt called to offer his own life for his people in a solemn ritual ceremony. [2]

It is generally granted now that the evolution of a higher culture in the near east began with the development of agriculture and irrigation under religious auspices, and that the rise of the city was a religious endeavor rather than a movement purely economic in inspiration. Men learned to make the earth fruitful, to raise flocks and herds through a cultic rite in which they cooperated with the hierophant or religious seer, hoping thus to re-enact the cosmic mystery of the fertilization and growth of nature. The annual repetition of the drama of the mother goddess and her maturing, dying, and reviving spouse or son was a recognition of the economic cycle of plowing, seed sowing, and harvest. Even the domestication of animals and the earliest agricultural organizations seem to have had their origins in a ritual observation and an imitation of nature that characterized what is known of pre-civilization religion.

At the prelude of history—the fourth millenium B.C.—Babylonia had already developed a specialized theology connected with its temple ceremonies. In the sumerian pantheon the gods and goddesses of each city had their special setting, and the people recognized their individual characteristics and personalities. The gods were the rulers of the city, and the king served as their representative and mouthpiece. The sumerian god or goddess owned the land, and presided over trade and banking; and the civil servants and administrators were the employees of the god. This was not a mere myth created by a state religion; it was rather the belief of the people

---

[2] See the reference to this practice in the I Epistle of Clement to the Corinthians 55; cf. A. Ziegler, "Auswanderung," *Neue Studien zum ersten Klemensbrief* (Munich, 1958), 95-101.

whose whole existence was communitarian, sharing the life of
the divinity.

With the rise of the successive dynasties of Babylonia and
Egypt in the next millenium, however, it is evident that a
series of intellectual and moral problems made themselves felt.
There arose a criticism of life itself and an intense spiritual
ferment that is captured by the egyptian author of the *Dialogue
of One Weary of Life* as he reflected on his own soul. Something similar was captured in the poetry of the *Righteous Sufferer*,
who had all the characteristics of a babylonian Job. These
documents disclose an acknowledgement of the differences
between what is, and what ought to be, in the moral and
social order. Even the great monarchical dynasts are judged
by their achievements or failures according to their employment of human, personal power and responsibility.

Thus Amenemhet I (ca. 1950 B.C.) counseled his son :

> Fill not your heart with a brother; know not a friend. Make not
> for yourself intimates of whom there is no end. Harden yourself
> against subordinates, that you may be king of the earth and ruler
> of the lands; that you may increase goodness. [3]

By the fourteenth century B.C., Akhenaten attempted to
found a state religion for syrian Egypt in the form of a solar
monotheism with universal pretensions; he even tried to
discover the first principles and sources of the changing phenomena behind nature. But his endeavor was aborted as the
"pride of the criminal of Akhenaten" by the guardians of the
traditional theocratic religion of the Nile Valley.

A thousand years before the birth of Christ, a spiritual
mutation of universal proportions can be recognized in the old
world cultures. Its vestiges seem to lie beneath the immediately
prehistorical phases of all the emerging peoples from Persia to
China, and from India to the shores of the Mediterranean.
This revolution destroyed the old religious civilization and
induced a vast cultural change. It seems to have resulted

---

[3] Quoted in C. Dawson, *The Dynamics of World History* (New York,
1956), 117.

from an almost simultaneous discovery of a new universe of unchanging reality beneath the appearances of the world of nature. Both in India and in Greece there are evidences of a seeking after cosmic causes or realities, called variously *Atman*, the *Logos*, or the *One;* and these forces controlled or explained the continual flux in the world of phenomena. In the Brihad-aranyaka Upanishad (3.7) Atman is referred to as "the self who dwells in the earth, but is other than the earth." He is the "self, the inward ruler, the deathless one who dwells in the mind, but is other than the mind." While he remains "unseen, he sees; unheard, he hears; unthought of, he thinks; uncomprehended, he comprehends ... All else is full of sorrow." [4]

The consequence of this awareness is the desire of the wise man for deliverance from worldly things—a crossing over the bridge of death to rise from appearance to reality, from time to eternity. Thus the attitude of the man who cultivated wisdom should be essentially ascetic; and the brahmin tried to purge his soul through a socratic-like intellectual discipline, while the Rigveda preached bodily penance or *tapas*, that would lead to the "disciplines of salvation." Essentially this philosophy of self-denial lies beneath the movements of the Jains, Yoga, and the Way of the Buddha seeking Nirvana.

Despite the seeming difference between the terrestrial self-abnegation of the indian ascetic, and the hellenic attitude toward life, both the brahmin and the greek of Iona or Italy in the sixth century B.C. were seeking an identical end—a piercing of the clouds of appearances to grasp the reality behind them. The greeks began with the tools of rational inquiry; and a youthfulness of spirit led them on to the natural sciences. Later they were influenced by an orphic mysticism that caused an absorbing interest in the doctrines of rebirth and immortality. They sought a progressive release from the defilement of corporeal existence, hoping thereby to achieve a sensible enlightenment of the soul. This searching resulted in the sudden desire for a vision of eternity; it was best realized by Plato, who insisted on the relationship between the world

---

[4] *Ibid.*, 117-118.

of appearances and shadows, between passing phenomena and timeless reality.   In his discovery, however, he was indebted to immediate predecessors, who had been men of no small intellectual and observational ability, from Socrates to Solon and from Hesiod to the homeric authors.

It was from this hellenic people with their new blood, institutions, ideals, and spirit that the phenomenon of the *polis* or city-state took its rise, combining the practices of the oriental sacred city and the purposefulness of the indo-european warrior tribe.   This new spirit expressed itself in a religious *élan* and a devotion to scientific inquiry that achieved the adornment of the hellenic city with its splendid buildings and monuments, its ornate temples and their exquisite statuary. It likewise induced a strict discipline, and a sense of solidarity and kinship among the inhabitants, that was expressed in the search for a *rationale* of politics.

It is in this realm of political endeavor that the roots of western classical culture were developed; and on this foundation the judeo-christian adventure took its rise.   Later it was to influence the formation of a truly european civilization, and eventually affected the whole of the modern world. [5]

THE HOMERIC MAN

Homer inaugurated his magnificent meditation on the nature of man and of human destiny with the reflective comment:

> Muse, sing of the anger of Achilles,
> and of his strife with Agamemnon, Son of Atreus.
> Which of the gods set them to strife with each other?

Far from rhetorical, the question goes to the center of the epic that he is about to record; for the poet does not see events from within the consciousness of the human actor, as does the modern novelist.   His world was dominated from the outside by the gods; and while he described the great deeds and heroic attitudes of his characters engaged in mortal combat between

---

[5] C. Cochrane, *op. cit.*, 414-428. Cf. W. Jaeger, *Paideia* 1, 3-56.

individuals and whole peoples, his primary interests were more theological than political.

The homeric man was essentially an aristocratic figure who lived in a world of movement and continual challenge, and attempted to direct his experiences with both intelligence and ingenuity. Face to face with the mysteries of the world in which he found himself, his imagination discovered behind each object and each event a demonic force, while his reason struggled to give these forces an orderly explanation. He saw his destiny *(moira)* involved in his ability to overcome not merely the difficulties that cluttered his daily life, but the obstacles placed in his path by the unpredictable vagaries of the elements, and by the wilful political ambitions of other peoples. Thus he devoted himself to the heroic task of over-coming chance or necessity by means of his personal powers of virtue, and of conquering his adversaries by skill and craftiness or ingenuity. [6]

This was a prodigious undertaking, since the demonic forces he desired to cope with were at once innumerable and erratic. They appeared to him likewise as both personal, and thus capable of benign reactions to his efforts; or impersonal, and thus inconscient of his feelings, and incapable of being influenced or changed in their inexorable march.

Life for the homeric man was a series of perilous adventures in which success was possible only for the individual endowed by favorable chance *(tyché)* with manly excellence or virtue *(areté)*, and possessed of faith or self-confidence *(tharsos)*. For the "godlike" heroes described in the *Iliad* and the *Odyssey*, the world was on the whole good; and life was a series of adventures in which bravery and constancy were rewarded with exhilaration. Its only true drawback was the certainty of death, and the uncertainty of the world beyond the shades.

As a poet, Homer was superb in catching the tremendous scope of creation, as well as the immediacy of everyday life, and in reflecting the innumerable facets of his heroes' personality. But as a theologian and political philosopher—and for the

---

[6] W. Jaeger, *op. cit.*, 57-76.

ancient greek the two functions were all but identical, since they conceived "of all things as full of gods"—his perspective is limited too particularly to the world of the hero. In the *Odyssey*, however, there are indications that the sheer optimism characteristic of the *Iliad* is beginning to fade; in its place an attempt is made to understand the forces involved in every man's destiny.

It is this aspect of the homeric heritage that is worked over by Hesiod and Pindar, and by the athenian dramatists, who looked for an answer to the meaning of life in aesthetic rather than intellectual satisfaction. While they criticized the ideas of Homer, they utilized an ideology that was essentially homeric; and when the sheer force of their creative ingenuity spent itself in the cul-de-sac of necessity *(anagké)* that remained inexplicable despite their promethean efforts, greek tragedy exhausted itself among the successors of Euripides.

Meanwhile, on the practical level of daily life, the lawgiver arose to bring regularity into the current of human affairs; and after him the philosopher, who, in this ambiance, turned his attention to the study of politics as an art that Aristotle was to characterize as the highest of humane endeavors, since it dealt with the ordering of human affairs in a search for the fulfilment of man's true destiny.

With Hesiod the ideal of justice was introduced in the hellenic reflection on man's political activities. His *Works and Days* began with a prayer to Zeus, who brings the mighty low and exalts the humble, to defend the righteous. In his *Theogony* or the *Descent of the Gods*, Hesiod wrote as a constructive theologian, and juxtaposed ethical forces with the atmospheric and telluric powers of nature. This he accomplished by arranging the facts of myth, cult, and psychological experience into a history of the origins of the cosmos and the beginning of human life.

In a strikingly original poetic form, he employed both reason and imagination to explain the inevitability of toil and strife in human existence, and the presence of evil in the world. He felt that neither human labor nor enmity could have been part of the original divine plan; hence he introduced the rape of fire from heaven by Prometheus as a sufficient reason for the divine anger that Zeus exercised in creating the scheming Pandora, the first woman. Through her curiosity, innumerable evils were loosed upon mankind, from hunger and fear to sickness and old age. [7]

In a second consideration of the perversity that man meets with in the world, Hesiod used the myth of the golden age, and of four subsequent stages of human degeneration, as he blamed the increase of human unhappiness on *hybris*, a combination of arrogance and folly. This vice had caused reverence for the gods to disappear, and had brought war and violence into such prominence that in the mind of the conqueror, *might is right*. In protest, Hesiod told the fable *(ainos)* of the hawk and the nightingale. While carrying this exquisite, though feeble creature in his talons, the bird of prey advised her not to complain, for "I can eat you or let you go, as I wish."

Hesiod's answer to this degeneracy in human affairs was a return to justice; and in contrasting the just and unjust city, he cited instances of the blessings that accompanied righteous activity, and the curse that followed evildoing. To give his moral presuppositions substance, he personified *diké* or justice as an independent divinity, the daughter of Zeus. Here his religious and moral enthusiasm seemed to be inspired by the serious attitudes toward life that he discovered among the rising class of peasants and townsfolk. Whether it reflects his actual experience or not, the realism of his achievement resides in his connecting the virtue of justice with the necessity of work. He thus created a practical ideal whose roots gave it substance, and whose appeal has been adduced in educational endeavors down through the centuries:

> It is easy to achieve misery even in crowds; that way is smooth and it runs close by. But the gods have ordered sweat before achievement. The path to it is lengthy and steep; and it is rough at first. Yet once the top is reached, the road becomes easy despite its difficulties.

---

[7] *Works and Days* 286; cf. W. Jaeger, *op. cit.*, 70. The similarity between Zeus bringing the mighty low, and Jahweh's similar activity, as well as the Eve-Pandora parallellism, has frequently been noted.

The habit or attitude that would achieve this functional competence was *areté*—virtue considered in its original sense. This included both ability and its use in achieving personal welfare, success, and good repute. Thus Hesiod concluded that man could not achieve his goal by violence, strife, or injustice. Once a man accepted this fact, he could be taught how to find the way to the good life.

With Hesiod the stream of greek intellectual consciousness accepted a type of spiritual leadership that did not claim competence because of noble birth or public office. Rather leadership was based on superior insight that reflected the *spiritus* or breath of God within a man; and on this score he has frequently been compared to the jewish prophets. As a poet-prophet with a deep insight into the divine plan for the world, he sought to lead erring men to the path of justice, and thus to peace and harmony. Despite his preoccupation with the peasant and the townsman, their folklore and unheroic ideals, he created a political philosophy that reflected a theological ordering too idealistic to be effective in a power-conscious society. But his rational approach to the significance of human desire and action prepared the way for the subsequent interest of the greek philosophers in theoretical as well as practical politics.

Hesiod represented the transition between the old order, in which the aristocrat and the peasant lived in a rural society, and the development of the culture of the city or *polis*, in which a true politics became possible. During the period that intervened between the close of this intermediary feudal society and the creation of the macedonian experiment in world empire by Alexander the Great, the city-state was the center of political development and the social framework for the whole of greek culture and life.

Like Hesiod, Solon had placed his political faith in the power of *diké* or justice, which is an inseparable part of the divine order. He excoriated avarice and selfish ambition as unjust, and he predicted that these vices would eventually lead to a visitation of divine anger, demanding full punishment for man's hybris.

"Driven by avarice," he warns, "the leaders of the people enrich themselves unjustly; they spare neither the goods of the state nor the temple treasures; and they neglect to preserve the sacred foundations of *diké*—who in her silence knows all the past and all the present. She does not fail to come in time to punish" (frag. 3). [8]

But unlike Hesiod, Solon saw this punishment in the disintegration of the state rather than in divine visitations of famine and pestilence; for every transgression of justice constituted a disturbance of the social organism. It manifested itself in feuds and civil war; and no citizen could escape this epidemic that "leaps over the high walls" of the city to visit every one of its doomed members. His diagnosis is based upon prophetic vision; it is a statesman's recognition of the facts. His antidote was *eunomia*, the concept of justice through the rule of law. It represented the first clear concern with a principle of an immanent order in the course of nature and of human life. Solon's conclusions were based on his observation of the course of history run by numerous greek city-states on both sides of the Aegean; so that he was able to cite chapter and verse for the validity of his deduction that injustice brought tyranny, and led to the seizure of power by a despot, to the ruination of the individual's freedom.

> "If you have suffered for your weaknesses,
> do not blame the Gods!" Solon exclaimed.
> "You yourselves allowed these men to grow
> great by giving them power; and therefore
> you have fallen into shameful servitude." [9]

This observation is a development upon the homeric theodicy that traced human misfortune more directly to the interference of *até* or the inevitability of fate arranged by the gods. Solon insisted that human responsibility played a great part in man's destiny, which was set indeed by immanent laws; but if those laws were recognized and obeyed, men could avoid disaster and final defeat. In an elegant prayer to the Muses, he maintained that man's natural impulse to possess could

---

[8] *Frag.* 3.6f : cf. W. Jaeger, *op. cit.*, 136-149; A. Ehrhardt I, 20-54.
[9] *Frag.* 8.

and should be curbed; and that wealth must be gained justly,
otherwise:

> The retribution of Zeus falls rapidly as
> a tempest in spring... it lets no one escape.
> One man makes amends soon, another late.
> If the guilty man escapes punishment
> his innocent children and descendants
> will suffer in his stead. [10]

It is out of this doctrine that the human experience of attic
tragedy was to arise a century later.

Meanwhile, however, the early hellenic thinkers had also
turned their minds to the nature of the material universe in
which they found themselves. In this, with their naturally
inquisitive and rational instincts, these men utilized the
technical skills and discoveries made by the people of Egypt
and the near eastern countries, in navigation, surveying, and
astronomy. By subjecting the myths and stories of creation
to natural reflection in the light of what they ultimately knew
about the physical world, the greek pre-socratic philosophers
made the first maps of the earth, and created scientific
geography. They thus arrived at a world picture that possessed
metaphysical profundity and structural unity.

In quick succession, Anaximander structured the universe,
and Pythagoras adduced the principle that number is the key
to the geometrical symmetry of the cosmos; but his further
speculations on the transmigration of souls has puzzled the
modern investigator. However, a new experience turned
greek attention to the inner structure of the human soul. This
was the orphic movement, whose influence on late antiquity
has been exaggerated, but whose discoveries introduced a new
consciousness of the self, and a new feeling for human life.
As a creed it had great moral significance, for in maintaining
that the soul came from God and is immortal, man had to be
interested in the preservation of the soul's moral integrity. For
the accomplishment of this ideal, orphic theology prescribed

---

[10] *Frag.i.* 17-32.

an ascetic type of self-restraint, including abstinence from animal food.

In contrast to orphism, there likewise arose the cult of the god Dionysius, apparently in response to a human need for spiritual as well as emotional excitement. Both these religious movements were somehow linked together in the worship of the delphic oracle, in which Apollo was pictured as insisting upon order, clarity, and moderation in human affairs. His teachings were expressed in a series of gnomic or pithy sayings that were considered a reflection of divine wisdom. Thus a new spiritual dimension was introduced into human affairs that gave rise to the search for philosophical knowledge, physical science, and political skill; but it had to be utilized also in the repression of individualistic impulses to wantonness that formed the sin of "not thinking human thoughts." The anodyne for such folly was the appolonian axiom *gnothi seauton*—know yourself. The virtue thus to be acquired was *sophrosyné* or wisdom.

Driven by the need for human happiness, the greeks had sought to escape from the perils of fortune that seemed as changeable as the weather, by a retreat into the inner world of their own souls, either in the self-forgetfulness of dionysiac intoxication, or in the orphic teachings about the development of man's spiritual powers. To avoid the awful aspects of a universal law, whose existence was symbolized in birth and death, and whose insistence on a vindictive justice was inescapable, they turned to a belief in a divine destiny. They became confident that on passing beyond the grave, the truth by which they had lived on earth would enable them to proclaim, "I, too, am of divine descent." This motto was inscribed on orphic gold plates and buried in southern Italy as a passport to life beyond the grave. [11]

In support of this belief, Xenophanes of Colophon, influenced by the natural philosophy of his contemporaries, attacked the old gods of the homeric world as ridiculous, since they were but anthropomorphic conceptions. He rejected them as useless in explaining man's final destiny. Instead, he attempted to create a new culture based on the philosophy

[11] W. Jaeger, *op. cit.*, 150-184; A. Ehrhardt I, 39ff.

that had replaced Homer's theogony with a natural and logical explanation of things. His concept of god is of one important being who lives beyond the universe, and who governs by pure thought, as he exists unmoved. This god is honored by the practice of true *areté* or virtue arrived at through the pursuit of philosophical truth; and this activity will benefit the *polis* more than any accomplishment in sports or other types of physical prowess. It is through intellectual power that man arrives at justice and law, right order, and welfare for the *polis* or city. Xenophanes thus brought together all the virtues that constituted the authentic *areté*—courage, prudence, justice, and finally wisdom. [12]

This summation provided an opening for the final stage of greek cultural development. While it insisted on the essential service of knowledge that Parmenides would assert to be the highest good in his discovery of the laws of logic, it likewise commanded the pursuit of decency and goodness. Heraclitus of Ephesus completed the cycle by asserting "Learning does not teach men to have sense"; and he then proceeded to plumb the depths of his own soul to find the source of the individual's speech and actions. "Travel over every road, yet you cannot discover the frontiers of the soul—it has so deep a *logos*." So saying, he introduced the idea of *phronesis* or prudence, and put it on a level with *sophia* or wisdom. He connected the knowledge of being with insight into human conduct and values; and with self-awareness he included the pursuit of prudence and wisdom. [13]

Heraclitus conceived of the *logos* as alone capable of comprehending the divine *nomos*, the law by which all human laws are nourished. The *logos* is the mind, the organ that perceives the meaning of the cosmos; and this *logos* knows itself and its own place and effect in the scheme of the universe.

While the poets such as Pindar and Theognis, the tyrants, and the playwrights contributed much to the understanding of the culture and behavior of human nature, their witness to political development was summarized by Herodotus and

[12] Cf. W. Jaeger, *op. cit.*, 457, n. 85.
[13] Heraclitus, *frag.* 40 and 45; cf. W. Jaeger, *op. cit.*, 178-184.

Thucydides, the former as an historian, the latter as the first political philosopher.

But another movement intervened that had a tremendous effect on hellenic political thought, and that directly influenced the education of a majority of the early christian fathers. As W. Jaeger has pointed out, the sophists came into prominence with the educational system that dominated the fifth and fourth centuries B.C. This philosophy was aimed directly at political education in the sense of training citizens to serve the *polis*. These new teachers insisted, to begin with, that the old aristocracy of race be replaced by an aristocracy of intellect. But this immediately presented a problem as to where the man with an extraordinary intellect should fit into the new scheme of things. It was never quite solved by the greek city-states, for while a Pericles was able to dominate Athens at the beginning of the peloponnesian war in favor of prudence and intelligence, Socrates was sacrificed to the fearful athenian reactionaries in favor of mediocrity. [14]

The sophists had first gained prominence by insisting that *areté* should be founded on knowledge and experience, and an ability to communicate the certainty thus acquired by speaking convincingly and powerfully. In classical greek the politician is thus referred to as a rhetor or an orator. The word denoted both ability to communicate, and the message itself. Eloquence thus became the leading quality of *areté* for the sophist : it is not virtue in a moral sense, but versatility in moving an assembly of citizens for the good of the *polis*.

In their educational procedures the sophists had returned to the poets, to Homer, Hesiod, Solon, Theognis, and Pindar. They regarded Homer as an encyclopedia of all human affairs, from saving one's soul to the building of wagons, and from navigation to strategy, while they held up his heroes as supplying a mine of providential knowledge for the conduct of life. Through the sophists, who exercised their trade as itinerant philosophers and teachers, the greek *paideia* or education came into being. It was to be the foremost element

---

[14] W. Jaeger, *op. cit.*, 286-331. A. Toynbee, *Greek Historical Thought* (New York, Mentor, 1952), 31-43.

in hellenic culture and education for almost a thousand years, and would influence the new christian religion both in the preparation of its great thinkers and teachers, and even enter into the christian theology. Christ himself would be considered by the greek fathers of the church as the foremost and model *pedagogue*.

In the transmission of political philosophy, it is to Thucydides that one must look for the beginning of the great empirical tradition that stands behind the theories of the later philosophers as they turned their mind to ethics and to politics. Herodotus was the first truly great historian of antiquity, but he did not enter the political arena as such. Euripides had denied that there existed any true *historia*, by which he meant the calm investigation of any "unchanging" object, other than natural or physical science. In political life he considered *historia* impossible, since the actors were constantly beset by hatred and conflict. Thucydides accepted the challenge, and by transferring the process of *historia* to political development, he gave a new and deeper sense to the search for truth. He defined the purpose of his work as not centered on mythology : "but it will suffice if it is judged useful by all who wish to study the plain truth of the events that have happened, and that will, according to human nature, recur in much the same way." [15]

Thucydides frequently expressed his conviction that history, both as regards individuals and nations, repeated itself because human nature does not change. This idea runs counter to modern concepts of history; it is likewise opposed by the judeo-christian conviction that from creation to the *eschata*, or "last things," there is a progressive unfolding of God's presence in history that reached its climax with the appearance of Christ, and that is still pulsating in a linear or spiral fashion through the experiences of the people of God in history.

While concentrating on individual events for their own sake, Thucydides attempted to pass beyond them so as to achieve a knowledge of universal experience, and the permanent laws therein contained. He thus raised a problem

[15] Thucydides, 1.22.4; cf. W. Jaeger, *op. cit.*, 388-390.

that the historian and political scientist still struggle to solve. The politician or statesman in particular must believe that in like situations, like causes are followed by similar effects. Otherwise it becomes impossible for him to plan. However, the history of mankind demonstrates that, whereas there is a basic identity to human nature in all individuals, and a similarity in political ambitions and strivings, these elements can be so combined in various fashions that there is almost an infinite variety of possibilities in political happenings; and yet the exceptional statesman can so utilize his knowledge of these possibilities, and his grasp of a particular situation, as for all practical purposes to predict or prepare for the next stage in history.

PLATO

In the *Laws* Plato showed an appreciation of these facts as he tried to trace the principal ideas that had gone into the thought of the early poets discoursing on politics. On the level of ideals, he traced *areté* to justice, and described justice as a disposition of the soul, reflecting the divine equanimity that informed the good man's dispositions to prudence, fortitude, and temperance. With an obvious aristocratic prejudice, however, he prescribed a philosopher as the ideal ruler; whereas Aristotle advised that the king should at least have a philosopher as his spiritual director or principal consultant.

On the practical level, Plato found that there were two principal ideas behind the development of hellenic political culture. One was the constitutional state represented by the evolution of ionian ideals; the other, the military cohesion and communal consciousness achieved by Sparta. Both experiences represented political and spiritual ideals that differed substantially. The spartan experience concentrated on education; the ionian on the development of philosophical and ethical truths that reached their climax in the Athens of the fifth and fourth centuries B.C. A coalition of both these experiences was elucidated in the platonic reflections of the *Republic* that combined the aristocratic influence of attic philosophy with the fundamental tenets of the ionian constitutional state, stripped of its democratic form.

ARISTOTLE

Aristotle had begun his reflections on the natural world with the principle that there was order in things. He postulated an immanent and discoverable relationship between the platonic concept of form and matter in finite existence; but he did so in such fashion as to avoid the dangers of Plato's transcendental idealism. He next envisaged man—*homo sapiens*—as disposed by nature to the achievement of *areté* or excellence in moving toward the purpose for which he existed. In man, this finality consisted in a hierarchical series of goods, after which he could strive. In the *polis*, he saw the possibility of an ordered society in which man best pursued these goods; and since man gave every indication of being a free-willed being, he must not only act purposefully, but he must be so organized in society as to have every opportunity of carrying out this teleology.

In the long run Aristotle insisted that the man who first invented the state was the greatest of human benefactors (*Polit.* 1.2.1253). He criticized both the athenian and spartan ideals as in the end unenforceable, and leading to tyranny; and he opted for an *autarchy* or self-contained state under the guidance of a single wise ruler who would be strong enough to allow the citizens an active part in their own governance. This is his ideal of the *polis*.

Aristotle avoided the cosmological analogies that Plato had introduced to illustrate his ideas of man's destiny in the *polis;* but he accepted his anthropology of body, soul, and mind. The latter, Plato had made the equivalent of a charioteer guiding the vehicle and horses to a common end. Aristotle further described man's destiny as bound in with the good life in the *polis*, where the citizen strove to achieve perfect order. That order was to spare man from the ravages of chance and accident. To prove this point Aristotle examined the constitutions of some fifty city-states, only to discover that none of them actually guaranteed true liberty whereby good men, intent upon achieving intelligent orderliness, could pursue the well-being of all. In the end, he criticized both democracies and oligarchies as favoring the lawlessness of the rabble, or the avarice of the rich.

Plato had set the date of the overthrow of the Areopagus in 461 B.C. as the beginning of the downfall of Athens, since it was with that outbreak that true religion or *aidos* had been openly repudiated. Aristotle maintained that the corruption had been manifest much earlier; he could see nothing but degeneration after the death of Solon, and while he admitted that Sparta had achieved a semblance of ordered civic life, he branded it as totally misdirected since it served a severely military ethos. [16]

Prescinding from the actual states with which he was familiar, Aristotle then laid out the lines of development for the ideal state whose end was the achievement of justice. He limited the size of the state to an area and population capable of sustaining itself economically, and in this regard he declared slavery natural. Next, he called for an organized militia, and the regulation of religious thought and emotion by an official priesthood. Finally, he set up a code for distributive and retributive justice. All this could be sustained by means of an education that would ensure all citizens a practice of moral and intellectual virtue, in keeping with the constitution that he characterized as based upon right thinking or orthodoxy. Thus he introduced a religion consisting of the worship of a truly political god, such as was preached by the delphic oracle of Apollo, as the only assurance of achieving justice, freedom, and peace in the *polis*. [17]

ALEXANDER THE GREAT

What seems ironical is that Aristotle's prescription for the perfect city-state was elaborated at the moment when a new

---

[16] W. Jaeger, *op. cit.*, Vol. II, 258-278. A. Ehrhardt I, 65ff; 125-128.

[17] A. Ehrhardt I, 127ff; cf. C. Hignett, *A History of the Athenian Constitution* (Oxford, 1952).

type of political organization was about to be born—the world state or *oikoumene*—a vast empire linking east and west under the tutelage of a man educated to feel himself destined to bring true order into his world. Besides the masterful planning that achieved his military prowess, Alexander the Great was determined to unite the territory he had conquered. He set about so doing by establishing metropolitan centers at strategic commercial points, from Egypt and the Caspian Sea, to the Danube and the Gulf of Persia; and he persuaded the greeks to emigrate to these new locations, bringing their language and culture with them. He likewise encouraged racial assimilation through marriage with the natives of the east, and set up military schools in which greeks and persians competed for knowledge and aptitude.

As a philosopher, finally, Alexander proclaimed the law of *philanthropia* or love of one's fellowman, to be demonstrated particularly in the case of the weak and downtrodden as an exercise of divine nobility. He himself accepted the role of *soter* and *euergetes* or savior and benefactor, in the concept of oriental kingship. But he found it difficult to have his macedonian and greek compatriots agree to perform the *proskynesis* or prostration when entering his presence. Nevertheless, the idea was transported to the west and would come into use with the gradual divinization of the ruler of the roman empire.

With Alexander's sudden death, the universal empire he had achieved was dissolved. However, he had transformed the political structure of the near east, and had uprooted the deep-seated immobility of ancient ethnic traditions. He had likewise forced the jewish people into the stream of world politics. [18]

CICERO

Meanwhile, the early roman conquests of the east had begun to intertwine, and gradually the dream of a single

---

[18] Cf. E. Barker, *op. cit.*, 1-19.

empire connecting the two great masses of the ancient world, projected by Alexander, was brought to actuality by the romans under Caesar and Augustus. To accomplish this herculean task, however, it was necessary to accept a radical change in the roman system of government that in fifty years developed from a turbulent republic into the principate of Octavian, and quickly took on the trappings of an empire. Several historians, such as Polybius, have described the political evolution that was in progress in the ancient world leading to this consummation. But the philosophical and religious principles that were to have the greatest effect upon christian political thought were epitomized by Cicero, partly in reaction to the factual situation, and in part by way of providing a refutation for the religious and civic nihilism advocated by Lucretius in his *De natura rerum*—on the nature of things.

To the anarchy that afflicted the roman scene in the last half of the first century B.C., Lucretius had tried to provide an answer by the merciless subjection of every philosophical and religious presupposition to the bar of reason. He thus branded as the source of all superstition the traditional gods of popular and poetic paganism. His answer was a return to absolute realism in the philosophy of Epicurus, and the doctrine of *atarxia* or detachment from religion and value judgment. [19]

Cicero attempted to provide an answer to the nihilism that he saw in the lucretian approach. He agreed that the tool had to be the use of *ratio*—reason—which he defined as that by which the society of men with one another is made possible and the community of life is held together (*De off.* 1.7.20). But the purpose behind this use of reason was to constitute the link between man and god (*De nat. deorum* 2.22.28). Man's destiny is linked with the formation of a society striving toward good and honest living; and in keeping with the historical development of the roman empire, Cicero changed perspective from the *polis* to the *res publica;* from the city-state to the republic.

A synthesis of roman political thought is thus furnished by

---

[19] *Ibid.*, 181-184; C. Cochrane, *op. cit.*, 35ff.

Cicero. In his *De officiis* he described the ideal attitude of the citizen whereby he could achieve the full usage of his native powers. Using terminology borrowed from the stoics, Cicero delineated human nature in its fundamental appetites and impulses, striving for fulfilment. He began with the urge to self-preservation and reproduction. These drives are the basic reasons for man's determination to defend himself and his possessions; and they are the final criterion in his avoiding what is harmful, while he searches for what will give him the assurance of goodness and satisfaction.

Beyond these fundamental considerations of human awareness, Cicero also found in man an inclination to social life for the purpose of communication and mutual assistance—*orationis et vitæ societas*. In his identification of himself with his fellowmen, the individual also finds the need to use his powers of reason in the search for truth—*veri inquisitio*—and in a desire for knowledge—*et scientiæ cupiditas*. Finally, there arises the determination to achieve prominence and appreciation.

Cicero asserted that the indulgence of this desire for excellence in society, whose fulfilment lies in the acquisition of superior knowledge or power, could only be justified if a man used it for the common good. This would lead him to a love for justice, and an orderly way of life in society. Moderation in word and deed—*decorum* or *prepes*—thus acquired, is the basis for his appreciation of beauty and harmony in the universe, as well as in human affairs.

It was his roman heritage that brought Cicero to insist upon man's final good as connected with the achievement of corporate security and social welfare in the organized community that is the state. While he discussed the individual man's desire to achieve wisdom, his natural tendency toward contemplation, and his urge to display courage and strength of mind, Cicero maintained that all these virtuous achievements should be marshaled in the service of justice. He thus broke with the true stoic ideal that saw man's purpose as fulfiled in the contemplation of the true, the good, and the beautiful. This ideal Cicero felt was rather a bonus than a right; and descending at once to the realm of the practical, he asserted that property was a fundamental concern of the man who is dedicated to the pursuit of justice in society. He found that property rights were based on peaceful occupation, conquest, agreement, or allotment.

He likewise maintained that the purpose of civil society as the embodiment of justice must be directed toward enforcing rights and restraining injustices by punishing the delinquent. However, he also held that the individual in society had two basic obligations : that of respect for the sanctity of a contract—*rerum contractuum fides*—since the mutual services men perform for each other are necessary in social life; and that of giving each man his due—*suum cuique tribuere*. This brought him to the observations that the acquisition of property and wealth had its limits, beyond which the desire to possess became avarice or greed for power, and destroyed both the soul of the individual and the fabric of justice in society. He thus commented on the "unsocial" money-making cupidity that characterized Caesar and Crassus, leading both to imperialistic visions, and a miserly fear of incurring personal expenses.

Going beyond Aristotle, who confined his application of the principles of justice to a manageable *polis*, and seemed to leave international relations to expediency or force, Cicero condemned the use of force, and prescribed the settlement of differences between nations by discussion and debate. He thus laid down a basis for international law, justifying the employment of arms only in cases where redress for probable injustice could be obtained in no other fashion. Even then he maintained there must be a formal declaration of intent and a warning. He likewise denounced the desire for national aggrandizement through conquest; and he distinguished between military effectives and non-combatants, while he maintained that the rights of individuals had to be respected. Finally, with regard to slaves, Cicero accepted the theory of the stoic Chrysippus that they should be considered and treated as permanent hired employees.

In the comportment of the citizen, Cicero looked for the practice of prudence, based upon the other cardinal virtues of justice, fortitude, and temperance. And he applied these criteria to the conduct of the state by the governor and the magistrates, with each citizen consciously accepting his proper station along with its duties. He thus discussed rules for decency in speech and behavior, and he compiled a catalogue of the occupations proper to the gentleman; these included education, medicine, architecture, commerce on a large scale, and agriculture; while the pursuit of politics and statesmanship was at once the noblest and the most dangerous of human occupations. He cited the lust for ascendancy—*libido dominantis*—and the desire for distinction—*appetitio principatus*—on the part of Caesar and Crassus as obvious examples of this peril.

In the end he maintained that justice was the fundamental consideration, making it more important than the acquisition of knowledge or wisdom. The western churchmen—and in particular Lactantius, Ambrose, and Augustine—were to be greatly influenced by the ciceronian attitude; and while each of them modified the application of Cicero's ideals in consideration of man's higher destiny, each recognized the basic truth in the roman political philosopher's observations. His insistence on the *jus gentium* and many of his *dicta* regarding human rights and obligations furnished much of the foundation for the doctrine of natural law that has been so prominent a consideration down to modern times.

In one other sphere Cicero's conclusions had considerable effect on the development of at least western christian political thought. He advocated an active and vigorous public opinion as the true safeguard of freedom and the guardian of justice in the republic—*consensus vel concordia ordinum;* and he maintained that this could only be achieved by conscientious leadership in the body politic. Once the christian community felt itself an organized entity, these considerations came into play. They were not necessarily approached in ciceronian terms; but in the west in the fourth century and thereafter, they were a strong factor in the pursuit of the christian way of life.

While Cicero had discussed the ideals of justice, and the proper forms that should characterize a true republic, he had criticized Cato for speaking as if he lived in a *platonopolis*—a platonic city—instead of in the *sarcina* or cesspool that was the Rome founded by Romulus. Consequently Cicero's final conclusions dealt not with the problem of liberty and monarchy in the roman state, but rather, in full realism, with what form the monarchy should take.

Augustus settled that problem in the practical order. He achieved a *pax augusta*, in the phrase of Velleius, the retired army officer who wrote "in the days of Tiberius Caesar," and left posterity an authentic picture of how the accomplishment of the Caesar—Octavian become Augustus—had affected the thinking of his world.

What is more, Octavian, in mobilizing his forces against Anthony and Cleopatra, represented himself as the champion of latin civilization against the sinister east. Once final victory was achieved, the emperor turned to Virgil in particular to draw the lesson of his attempt to renew the total life of the empire by a return to the ideals of the ancient roman state. And Virgil complied by describing in his *Aeneid* the magnitude and the dangers of the task that the augustan progress had undertaken. Virgil depicted on the shield of Aenaeus the final battle between the decadent forces of Anthony and the shameless egyptian woman, Cleopatra, and the armed might of Italy's fathers and sons, who were arrayed against these barbarians. He typified the final issue as a contest between the austere latin state with its household deities, and the foul demons of the oriental imagination; the yelping Anubis and the monstrous gods of Egypt against Neptune, Venus, and Minerva (*Aeneid* 8.675ff). [20]

The accomplishment of Augustus in restoring a *concordia nova* to the empire, and his providential proclamation of a universal *pax romana*, was to be considered by future christian thinkers as directly the work of almighty God's deliberate action in history. Virgil described his destiny as given to *parcere subjectis* and *deballare superbos*—to spare his subject peoples and dethrone the proud. The augustan policy fitted in with Old Testament thinking, and would be one of the primary reasons

---

[20] C. Cochrane, 38-76; A. Ehrhardt, 258-302.

why the civil authority was invested with power, in St. Paul's thought (Rom 13,1-7). Likewise Augustus had served as the protector of civilization not merely by defining the limits of the empire, but by linking the vast expanse under his governance with roads and bridges, and the despatch of trained soldiers and magistrates to administer justice everywhere.   This achievement impressed itself upon the later christian imagination, and became the source of legend as well as a model of political righteousness all through the middle ages.

2

The Hebrew Background

The religion of Israel was that of a nomad, warrior people that in the first millenium B.C. had occupied a limited territory in the near east, and was neither rich nor highly civilized. Yet despite their material insignificance, this people had managed to gain a foothold among the older nations of the eastern mediterranean basin, retain their integrity, and become the instrument of a higher religious tradition. The God of Israel was not a deity of the city like Baal of Tyre, nor an agricultural divinity like Tammuz. He was a god of storm and battle, who came up from the desert or down from the hills to destroy his enemies and judge his people (Hab 3,1-6).

The hebrew religion had its roots in a solemn covenant or *berith* by which the nation had become the people of God. Whereas the other semitic tribes looked to their god primarily as their king, the israelites turned to him as their father. In the early hebrew tradition there is no attempt at philosophical or political speculation as such, nor is there any evidence of a movement to transcend the social order, or to deny the obvious meaning of the temporal and historical process.

The God of Israel was a jealous god who proclaimed his living presence among his people, and forbade them to consort with the surrounding populace's deities, or to participate in the fertility rituals of Assar and Ishtar, of Chemosh the god of Moab, or of Astharoth. Instead, the religious and moral life of both the individual and the organized society in Israel was based on a ritual order. The sacred city of Jerusalem and its priesthood were presided over directly by the Word, and governance of a personal divinity, Yahweh, the God of Israel. [1]

By the eighth century B.C., and the earliest prophetic writings, Yahweh was considered much more than a merely national deity. For Amos he was the god "who made the Pleiades and Orion, and changed darkness into morning, and made day over into night" (5,8). He formed the mountains, and he controlled the sea, and he revealed his desires to man; he despised the sacrifices of those who exploited the poor, and took no pleasure in the external observances of the national cult. His law was "to leave evil and love the good, and to establish judgment in the gate" (*Ibid.* 9-18).

The misfortunes of Israel were the result of Yahweh's wrath, and every political crisis was a reminder for Israel to return to the laws of Yahweh and to renew the terms of the *berith* or covenant. In the writings of the prophets, the successive misfortunes of the hebrew people were new occasions for further revelations concerning this divine vocation; and gradually the visions of the prophets were extended beyond the kingdom of Israel to the nations, dynasties, and world empires that continually threatened their integrity and very existence.

When Assyria overpowered the nations of the east, and the hebrew peoples were sent into exile, the prophets of Israel saw in the material calamity of the nation not the powerlessness of Yahweh in preserving his people, but a manifestation of his mysterious designs. Assyria was pictured as but an instrument of the God of Israel; it would be discarded when its purpose was fulfiled.

Gradually this judgment of Yahweh was also extended against the nations, and was visited upon injustice and the pride of men. Isaiah described the Day of the Lord of Hosts who descended upon "everyone who is low" in terms that echo Hesiod and Solon (Is 2,12-17).

---

[1] Cf. J. Pedersen, *Israel, Its Life and Culture* (London, 1926-1940); W. Irwin, "The Hebrews," *The Adventures of Ancient Man* (Chicago, 1946), 322-333; H. Renckens, *The Religion of Israel* (New York, 1966); C. Dawson, *Progress and Religion* (New York, 1938), 155-163.

By the mid-second century B.C. these prophetic utterances had been developed into an apocalyptic and political doctrine, as can be seen in the two famous visions in the book of Daniel: the one based on the dream of Nebuchadnezzar (Dn 2,31-45); and the other on the dream of Daniel (7,1-14). The statue of the king's dream, with head of gold and its parts, in descending order, of silver, bronze, iron, and iron mixed with clay, was destroyed by an immense stone that no human hand had released, but that had annihilated the statue and then grown until it filled the whole world. The author of the book of Daniel interpreted this dream as representing the four great kingdoms of history that were about to cease before a fifth that would last forever.

In the second dream, four beasts appeared in succession; and they were followed by a creature "like the Son of Man," to whom was given "dominion, glory, and a kingdom that all people, nations, and languages should serve. His reign is an everlasting dominion that will not be supplanted, and his kingdom shall not be destroyed." Originating in the middle of the second century B.C., when the seleucid kingdom was about to absorb the jewish nation, these dreams expressed clearly the messianic hope of the jews. When Palestine was finally conquered by the romans, the enmity against foreign domination was transferred to this new roman "kingdom of wickedness."

Explanations of this prophecy are innumerable. It has long been recognized, however, that the author was writing in the mid-second century B.C., and that he synthesized a series of individual apocalyptic currents, giving rise to an anti-seleucid policy, that was turned against the subsequent domination of the hebrew and other near east peoples. The prophecy forms the foundation of the great outcry against the antichrist in the Apocalypse, and will be commented on as such by the roman priest, Hippolytus. Whether it formed part of an anti-roman, general, political movement is problematical. [2]

---

[2] Cf. J. Swain, "Theory of the Four Monarchies," *Classical Philol.* 35 (1940), 1-21; C. Dawson, *Dynamics of History* (New York, 1956), 253-254.

I.

On a lower political level, whatever may be the origin of the jewish ritual laws—and scholars are in disagreement over the very status of the problem—it is obvious that the lawgivers had gradually changed the original meaning of these rites in a progressive sense. In the course of primitive jewish history these archaic taboos and directives became an ethical code, reflecting a truly religious and spiritual doctrine. In Deuteronomy, the sabbath had a humanitarian and sacred meaning with emphasis on the well-being of the laborer and of his right to rest. The rites concerned with marital celebrations, the first-born's ceremonial welcoming, along with prescriptions for repose for the land, took on an authentic spiritual and ethical significance. Even circumcision was given a more spiritual interpretation in the later jewish documents. [3]

With the prophets there had been a definite reconsideration of the more intimate values of the jewish religion. Amos, Isaiah, Jeremiah did not hesitate to criticize the whole idea of sacrifice that seemed to be an essential factor in the earlier jewish religious practice. And in the Torah there was a development and a change of mentality that gradually insisted on a religion "in spirit and in truth" (Am 5,21; Os 6,6; Mi 6,7). Jeremiah had spoken of the circumcision of the heart rather than the flesh (4,4).

Despite these cautions, the legalist traditions of the hebrews had been codified in the Torah, which actually had a providential function in jewish history. It formed the people of God, then protected them from contamination. The law made men recognize that they were sinners; but it put them constantly in contact with God. It did not, however, give them truth, nor did it guarantee them a sharing in worldly justice.

For Plato in the *Republic*, justice had meant a perfect hegemony of the state, both civic and personal, so that the

---

[3] Cf. H. Renckens, *The Religion of Israel* (New York, 1966).

higher faculties commanded, and the lower members performed their functions fully and freely, each keeping to the activity assigned it by the governor or lawgiver. The law that established this order was the law of God as proposed and implemented in creation by his law of nature. This notion was accepted by Philo Judaeus, the early first century A.D. jewish philosopher and theologian of Alexandria, who maintained that justice could only be achieved by an inner adjustment, brought about through man's receiving a new augmentation from the divine spirit or *logos*. [4]

This contemplation of the law in the Torah thus brought a spiritual wisdom, and this Philo referred to as peace, harmony, virtue, salvation, or other virtue that he distinguished as a facet of the *logos* or divine wisdom *(sophia)*. Virtue, then, was an inner state of the mind in which one lived, guided by and in harmony with God and the *logos*.

Similar to the personification of virtue by Socrates in the *Symposium* of Plato, virtue is depicted by Philo in the allegory of Rebecca, who gave men to drink of her beauty if they were seeking higher values than mere sense perception. This quality in Rebecca began as virtue but soon turned into *sophia*, which is a gift that streamed from God and absorbed all human distinctions of value: namely, justice, bravery, self-control, and intelligence, together with the virtue of piety. [5] The ideal man was explained as the *nomos empsychos*, the *lex animata*, or law personified. It was the incarnate representative of supreme and universal law. In it the unformulated law is vocalized—it becomes the *logikos*. Thus the ideal man takes a law that is spirit or divine purpose, and applies it to human tribulations. It is through Moses, the ideal lawgiver in Philo's conception, that true law, which represents the nature of God, becomes statutory law for men in society. The bridge between the hellenistic concept of the origin of law, hence of the political continuum, and jewish ideology was explained by Philo in

---

[4] Cf. E. Goodenough, *An Introduction to Philo Judaeus* (Oxford, 1962).

[5] E. Goodenough, "Philo's Exposition of the Law," *Harvard Theol. Rev.* 27 (1933), 109-125; A. Ehrhardt, *Politische Metaphysik* I, 202-207.

his *Commentary on Creation* where he combined Plato's doctrine in the *Timaeus* with the mosaic narrative.

Philo utilized the two stories of creation in Genesis (1—2,3 and 2,4-25) to excellent advantage. The description of the creation in seven days that occupied the first chapter of Genesis is made the equivalent of Plato's conception of the pattern of the material world in the platonic world of ideas. This first creation was non-material and non-spatial; it existed in the *logos* or divine reason as in an architect's plan which was unfolded at first in his mind, without consideration of time or location. Hence the "days" of this creation represented merely order within the ideal world, and man is identified with the divine reasoning power through which he is the "image of God." Finally Philo accepted the use by God of secondary causes or assistants as did Plato, to avoid the problem of attributing to the divinity the cause of evil.

When he took up the second story of creation in Genesis, Philo asserted that here God respected the limitation engendered by time and space. The first man now is a combination of matter and spirit made from mother earth, but containing the image of God breathed into him by the *logos*. He is distinctively male, and a citizen of the world, a summation of the created universe, or a microcosmos. He is the very true king of all time. But his downfall began with the creation of woman who emphasized the material part of his nature, particularly awakening in him physical desire. Philo's final solution for the problematic of political behavior and law thus sought to combine the hellenistic and jewish concepts, and in this he would be followed by the christian fathers, beginning with Clement of Alexandria.

In the New Testament, Paul would be the theologian of the primitive church who described the process of spiritualization by means of a cleansing of the older jewish myths; and he brought the process of this evolution to a climax whereby judaism had its completion and perfection in christianity. In Deuteronomy, for example, circumcision served as a sign of mere obedience to God's law (10,16; 30,6). For Paul neither circumcision nor uncircumcision had any significance; what counted was the fulfilment of God's law (I Cor 7,14). He was looking for a thorough conversion to a spiritual evaluation of all of man's thinking and acting; and this, Paul maintained, the Torah could no longer achieve. It was God himself who made man holy and just; it was not obedience to the law as such, but faith in Christ Jesus: "For we maintain that man is justified by faith, and not by the work of the law" (Rom 3,28).

The law for Noah or for Abraham had been an act of holiness, an observance that brought man into the life of God, and sanctified his thinking and acting. For Paul, justification would be both the spirit and the life of man, and required a complete conversion, a radical renewal of his whole being (cf. Ez 36,26; Rom 8,3; Gal 3,21).

When Paul spoke of a law written in the hearts of the "gentiles" (Rom 1,26; 2,14), he did have reference to the law of nature *(physis)* treated in the current popular philosophy, but he was actually making it the equivalent of the Old Testament concept of the divinely created, concrete "nature" of man. In creation man was bound to an ethical law that was essentially comparable to the ethical constructs of the Torah. Paul was thus formulating a theology of history that is in keeping with Genesis (1 and 2), in which the foundations of the christian natural law had their inception. Augustine would accept this pauline concept and give it a threefold precisioning: a law given in paradise, naturally built into man's being, and only later promulgated in writing. It was thus the salvationary status of man before the coming of Christ that constituted the *ordo naturalis*, and that Augustine predicated of Cicero's concept: "Nature is that law, that is not a matter of opinion, but is inserted as a certain innate power; it manifests itself as religion, piety, grace, vindication [of rights], observances, and truth" (*De div.* 31).

II.

On one other political development, the jewish experience offered testimony both of its political significance, and of its ambivalent value in the conduct of human affairs. This was the matter of kingship. [6] Coming out of the mirage of pre-history onto the stage of the great world empires, the jewish people had a theocratic government; and by this they were ruled immediately through Moses and the judges and the prophets. But by contact with neighboring nations, they gradually succumbed to the desire for terrestrial status, and the security that the rule of a single house would afford them. With apparent reluctance, the God of Israel ceded to their request and founded the house of David. But he had warned through his prophets that their experience with kings would be no different from that of their neighbors, great and small.

Meanwhile, the prophets had also promised the coming of an age of final peace with a messiah; and the jews for the most part interpreted this promise in the sense of an earthly ruler. Their experiences with their own monarchy, and finally with that of the romans, had only served to increase the longing for this consummation. When Christ appeared, and gradually demonstrated his spiritual prowess, it was but normal that the majority of the jewish leaders should look upon him with suspicion. He possessed none of the qualities they associated with wordly domination, and with the magnificence of royalty that in their eyes would alone be sufficient to have him play a part in the tremendously complicated power politics of the roman empire into which they had been absorbed.

With Christ's apparent failure and crucifixion under the roman governor Pontius Pilate, the jewish leaders felt fully justified in their rejection of his claims. Thus they were taken aback to find his coterie of disciples continuing what they considered to be the subversive activities of founding a new sect; and they took measures to prevent the further spread of this aberration, as the Acts of the Apostles vividly attest. With the conversion of Paul, however, and the courageous activities of Peter and John and the other apostles, the effectiveness of

---

[6] Cf. L. Cerfaux et J. Tondriau, *Un concurrent du christianisme, le culte des souverains* (Tournai, 1957); E. Barker, "Essay on Kingship," *From Alexander to Constantine* (Oxford, 1956), 341-390.

the curbs used by both the pharisees and the herodian house was quickly broken; and christianity began its remarkable spread through all Judea and Samaria, then Syria, and Greece, and on to Rome.

The new christian church was to be considered by its own leaders and by the roman authorities as a continuation of the jewish ethnic group in the sense that its members were to be dealt with in the manner reserved for the jews by Julius Caesar and Augustus. According to Josephus, Caesar had legislated immunity from the imperial laws concerning religious cult for the jews, and he had allowed them to follow their "national customs and sacred rites." The imperial legislation down to the destruction of the temple of Jerusalem in 70 A.D. had guaranteed "their laws and freedom" (Jos. *Jew. antiq.* 14.195; 213; 260). After the destruction of the nation as a territorial entity, it survived as a religious community, or a *religio* that was recognized as *licita* by the roman authorities; it had its own national rights and liberties.

Once christianity manifested itself, however, there was sufficient reason for the confusion of the two groups in the estimate of the roman magistrates, for the early church inherited most of its formalities from the synagogue. The jewish "clergy" consisted of an *archisynagogus* or chief rabbi, priests, sacristans, lectors, and translators. All but the latter proved necessary in the christian church. The *archisynagogus* was the overseer *(episcopus)* of the community who presided at the divine liturgical service and instructed the people; the priests who had the power to bless, and who saw to the collection and distribution of the tithes; the sacristan who preserved order in the synagogue and provided for its material wants; and the lector who read the scriptures during the divine services.

St. Ambrose in the late fourth century, writing his commentary on Ephesians (4,11.12), pointed out the striking similarity between these offices and those found in the christian church (*PL* 17.387). Ambrose compared the functions of the *archisynagogus* and the christian bishop; the jewish priests and the christian deacons; and the sacristans and the masters *(magistri)* who kept order, particularly among the children—"as is the custom of the jews whose tradition has come down to us." [7]

This parallel had been reproduced in the general governance of the two communities. In the synagogue, a counsel of elders *(presbyteroi)*, usually with the *archisynagogus* as presiding officer, superintended financial affairs, passed judgment on the worthiness of the members, adjudicated disputes, and represented the community's interests in dealing with the civil authorities. Ambrose acknowledged explicitly a similar function on the part of the college of priests with the bishop in the christian churches, and traced its origin to this jewish organization. And just as the jewish councils judged the local religious disputes and expelled heretics, so were the christian bishops and the priests organized into independent meetings or synods to judge doctrinal disputes, acting locally as self-sufficient corporations.

This pattern would be likewise the basis for the church's development; for the christians took out of the synagogue with them the devotions, scriptures, liturgical music, hours of prayer, and feast days, as well as the sermon type of scriptural exegesis, the moral code, and above all the concept of sacrifice and oblation that had characterized jewish worship. This fact is obvious in the earliest christian documents, and was emphasized by the church fathers, who insisted absolutely on the continuity between the two religious observances.

Finally, on the more obvious, political level, the christians would also share the attitude toward the empire that had kept the jewish people from being absorbed into the roman state. The christians tended to consort together in separate, independent groups based on a sacramentally conceived "communion of belief." Their community was governed directly by the law of God; and it was superior to the law of man as expressed in the state. Besides, the local christian church belonged to a much wider community, that had God as its ruler.

---

[7] *PL* 17. 387. Cf. J. Schmitt, "Sacerdoce judaïque et hiérarchie ecclésiale," *Rev. Sci. relig.* 29 (1955), 58-71; J. Juster, *Les Juifs dans l'Empire Romain* (Paris, 1914), 450-456; G. Figueroa, *The Church and the Synagogue in St. Ambrose* (Washington, 1949).

The general jewish political attitude toward the roman state was taken over by the christian exegetes and, in consequence of instructions given to the jews by Jeremiah, and repeated for the christians by St. Paul, and the author of I Peter, christians would be told they had an obligation to pray for the empire and even the cruelest rulers.

The performance of such prayers followed the earlier jewish practice. From the time of Augustus at least, the jews had been allowed to offer sacrifices in the temple each day in the emperor's name. This was considered a satisfactory substitute for the sacrifice required by the roman cult to the genius of the emperor. After the destruction of Jerusalem, this sacrifice was replaced by prayers for the emperors in the synagogue, and this found its way into the primitive christian ritual.

Conscious, however, of its divine institution and its spiritual independence, in matters religious, from state control, the christian community would quickly be compelled to work out its own jurisdictional system to combat heterodoxy of belief, and to eliminate heretics from official positions as well as membership. Purity of faith would be inseparable from ecclesiastical jurisdiction; and only those who were established in the canon of the faith could judge whether a bishop had deviated from the true faith, and thus become unworthy of his office.

It is this exclusivism of faith leading to life as a new creature in Christ that would be made clear by the apologists of the second century, such as Aristides (*Apol.* 2), and the author of the *Keryma Petri*. There could thus be no confusing the christians with the devotees of the oriental religions who were spread throughout the roman empire; and still less with the stoics who proclaimed themselves citizens of the world, and also had a doctrine of brotherhood with all mankind. Actually, there was no possibility of identifying the christian with an adept of the mystic religion of Serapis or of Mithra. For the followers of these cults grouped themselves in confraternities or clubs, while the philosophers formed schools. But the christians would organize a church, of which the local community was consciously an immediate representation, but it would not seek national expression, nor strive for an independent political totality. In the third century, Origen would maintain that

> among us, believers come from one city or another, from one nation and another, without any group representing a whole people.
> It is not the same with christians as it is with jews or egyptians who form a nation or a race.
> Christians come from, and are, everywhere.
> (*In Ps.* 36, *Hom.* 1).

The Early Christian Experience

In a very real sense, the New Testament can be considered a political document or manifesto. For from the pedestrian description of the call of Matthew, the tax-gatherer, through the paradoxical commands of Christ to go one's neighbor one better—to turn the other cheek; importuned to go one mile, to go two—to the catalogue of everyday virtues in I Peter and the pastoral epistles, and the final tremendous display of the eschatological battle fought by the demons and the beast of the Apocalypse, the document is one long piece of propaganda. It is at once spontaneous and designed, anthropomorphic almost to a fault with the simplicity of biographical incidents in the life of Christ and the apostles; but it rises to a sophistication that leaves the mind reeling when Christ speaks of the relations between himself and his heavenly Father, or Paul discusses the height and the depth, and the breadth of the wisdom and knowledge of God (Eph 3,18). The implementation of the message contained in this document revolutionized the political thinking of the ancient and medieval world. Its implications in the reconstruction of modern civilization seem to be merely at the launching stage.

As portrayed in the gospels, Christ made no attempt to participate in the political activities of the roman empire, nor even in the local jewish hegemony of Palestine. He left behind him no legacy of political theorizing. But he did and said things that demonstrated his fundamental interest in the way human life was governed and lived; and in particular, in the poor man's lot, and the rich man's obligation to use his possessions in such fashion as to be a fit candidate for the kingdom of heaven. While it is obvious in his preaching that his kingdom is not immediately of this world, it does have a fundamental relationship to all that goes on in man's public and private life while he sojourns in the *paroikia* of this earth.

In all the documents dealing with early christianity, from the New Testament to the apologists of the second century, fundamental attention is given to the pursuit of virtue in the political context of a citizenship in the church, in what is called the *catechesis* or moral instruction. There is no direct theorizing concerning political principles as such, or of their implementation in historical circumstances, but there are strong overtones of political interest from the frequent references to "a king," "a strong man armed" of Christ's parables, to the civic structures, the sports, and military references and similes in the pauline epistles. [1]

In actual fact, Christ is depicted as having accepted the political order prevailing in Palestine "in the days of Caesar Augustus... when Herod was king in Judea" (Mt 2,1). As a child, and in the course of his public life, he obeyed the local temple rulers; he had Peter pay the didrachma of the temple so as "to avoid giving scandal" (Mt 17,26). When challenged by the scribes and pharisees to declare himself in regard to his position on the roman hegemony over Palestine, Christ wisely asked to see the coin of the tribute. In reference to Caesar's image and inscription thereon, he remarked: "Render unto Caesar the things that are Caesar's; and to God what belongs to God" (Mt 22,20-21).

That sentence rings down through the ages of christian political theorizing as a principle and a challenge; and it has had the most far reaching effects from the short petrine admonition (I Pt 2,11-17), and St. Paul's commentary in the epistle to the romans (13,1-20), through the writings of most of the

---

[1] O. Cullman, *The Early Church* (London, SMC, 1956), 195-209; W. Eltester, "Die Krisis der Alten Welt und das Christentum," *Zeitsch. Neutest. Wissenschaft* (1949), 1ff.

church fathers and the great theologians from Augustine to Aquinas, and from Martin Luther to John Calvin and Jacques Maritain. [2]

But this was not the only reference in Christ's life to the exigencies of practical politics. The evangelists are careful to connect his career with the reign of the roman rulers, from the beginning of his preaching "in the fifteenth year of the reign of Tiberius Caesar" (Lc 3,1) to his death on the cross "under Pontius Pilate," the procurator of Judea, a phrase preserved and recited daily in the Apostles' Creed. It was in conversation with Pilate, actually, that Christ made an explicit admission of his own kingship, though he was quick to add "but my kingdom is not of this world," (Jn 18,36) despite the fact that he had told the jews on several occasions that he was a king in Israel (Jn 19,21).

This circumstance was apparently not unknown to the romans, who placed a placard on the cross upon which he was crucified that read "Jesus Christ, King of the Jews" (Jn 19,19). Until "his time had come," however, he studiously avoided any action that might give the appearance of claiming temporal rulership in Israel; several times, the gospels report his sudden disappearance when the jews "sought to make him their king."

In dealing with both the temple and civil rulers, however, Christ generally showed himself decorous, if not deferential. He dined in the homes of the pharisees, cured the son of the centurion, and in the end accepted the rude and unjust condemnation of the high priest Caiphas and of the Sanhedrin. He had even instructed the people to obey the scribes and pharisees, explaining the law of God to them: "Everything they tell you, observe and do ..." (Mt 23,3). But this did not prevent him on occasion from excoriating those same leaders as hypocrites and pointing out their dishonesty and dissemblances. He drove the moneychangers out of the temple as both profaning the house of God and doing a disservice to the poor. Nor did he hesitate to rescue the woman taken in

---

[2] Cf. W. Muller, *Church and State in Luther and Calvin* (New York, Anchor, 1956); J. Maritain, *The Things that Are Not Caesar's* (New York, 1930).

adultery, or to refer ironically to Herod, calling him a sly fox.

The accusation that Christ refrained from committing himself to commenting on or righting the social disorders of his day is simply not true, *pace* Bertrand Russell and other modern critics. When questioned by the disciples of John the Baptist, as a matter of fact, he made an issue of that subject: "The blind see, the lame walk, and the poor have the gospel preached to them" (Mt 11,5). The reference was directed toward the prophecy of Isaiah, identifying the messiah to come; but the fact is that he did feed the poor, cured the unwanted sick, and consoled the exploited. Moreover, in speaking of the role to be played by his disciples in the world, Christ had been explicit in asserting their obligation to serve as a leaven for the spiritual uplift of mankind. "You are the salt of the earth," he informed them (Mt 5,3-16).

That he did not attempt to reorganize the political and economic structures of his age was due to another factor. He had a revolutionary task to fulfill, the redemption of the whole of mankind; and in comparison with that eschatological obligation, the structures of this world's society were but a passing fancy. In like manner he had come to found a church that would preach and spread the good news of the redemption to all nations, and have a political effect on the hegemony of the world to the end of time. To have enmeshed himself in the local political problems of the jews, and particularly in the fanatical activities of the zealots, would have compromised both his current, or temporal, and his otherworldly objectives. [3]

It is in this perspective that Christ's life and teaching have had a world-shaping character as far as political theory and practice are concerned. He showed himself conscious of the rest of the world on several occasions recorded by the evangelists, speaking well of the syrians and phoenicians, and assuring his disciples that "many would come from the east and the west and sit at the hand of God with Abraham, Isaac and Jacob" (Mt 8,11). But it was in the institution of the

---

[3] G. Kittel, *Die Probleme der palästinischen Spätjudentum und das Urchristentum* (1926); S. Baron, *A Social History of the Jews. Ancient Times* (2nd ed. New York, 1952).

church on the apostles after his resurrection that he declared: "All power in heaven and on earth is given to me. Go therefore and teach all nations, telling them whatever I have told you. And behold, I will be with you all days, down to the end of the world" (Mt 28,20).

While Christ's comportment vis-à-vis the civil authority was correct and at times even deferential, his preaching of the kingdom of God was from the beginning strictly in keeping with the eschatological tradition of the jewish prophets. Nevertheless, he avoided association with the political zealots who felt called upon to overthrow the roman rule in Palestine as essentially satanic in origin, and to restore a messianic kingdom modeled apparently on the older theocratic concepts. In dealing with his disciples, likewise, Christ forbade them to speak of him as the messiah when finally they began to realize the import of his mission (Mt 12,9).

There was thus in Christ's teaching and actions an ambivalence that goes to the very essence of the christian message. He and the church he founded were "in this world but not of it." But being in the world meant coping with its problems, and supplying answers that, while they have an unworldly ring, do have immediate if heroic meaning for everyday life. This message of Christ has been conveniently gathered together by Matthew in the Sermon on the Mount (Mt 5-7), where Christ is portrayed as explaining the law of God with otherworldly authority : "Of old it was said to you ... but I say ..." Later, Matthew portrays him as giving the source of his authority: "All things have been handed over to me by my Father. And no one knows the Father but the Son" (Mt 11,27).

While Christ condemned injustice and spoke of the final punishment of the wicked, the kingdom of God as he described it is rather a reign of the just, in which sinners are called to repentence (Lc 5,32; Mt 15,24; 20,1ff.), and where justice is to reign (Mt 25,21.23). It is a kingdom of glory (Mk 10,37), of life (Mk 9,43.45), and of light (Mk 16,18), for God himself is to reign there.

What distinguishes this announcement of Christ from the

older prophetic tradition is the fact that "the kingdom of God is at hand" (Mt 3,2); "it is among you" (Mt 4,11). Yet his followers are to pray daily: " Thy kingdom come" (Mt 6,10). The resolution of this dichotomy has exercised the ingenuity of countless exegetes, particularly in the last hundred years. What must be admitted is that it represents "the mystery of the kingdom of heaven," beginning with the direct intervention of Christ, the Son of God, in human affairs through his passion, death, and resurrection, and the sending of the Spirit on the first Pentecost. On the political level, Christ did not call for the abandonment of the things of this world; but he did put them in their proper perspective. "What good will it do a man if he gain possession of the whole world? . . ." (Mt 16,26), a not unrealistic consideration in view of very recent history. [4]

In one other sphere Christ's words and activities have had a fundamental bearing on political thought; that is in the story of his temptation by Satan. For in that encounter the mystery of the powers of evil that were credited with infecting political developments with war and catastrophes are given a preternatural explanation that, combined with his predictions concerning the world crisis that will precede the end of time (Mt 24,1-45), have challenged the spiritual exegete and the political philosopher to this day.

Christ was definitely speaking in terms of the beliefs of his age as he drove out devils and described the powers of Satan. For the whole world, hellenistic and roman, as well as barbarian, oriental, and jewish, believed explicitly in the power of demons. While modern skepticism in this regard calls for a demythologization, most particularly in this witness of the scriptures, it has little to offer in their place by way of accounting for the "wickedness in high places" that bedevils modern world affairs just as satanically as it did the roman world. Whatever be the sophisticated resolution of this problem, it immediately affected christian political thought

---

[4] Cf. O. Cullman, "The Kingship of Christ and the Church in the NT," *The Early Church,* 105-137.

with St. Paul, and above all with the witness of the Apocalypse or book of Revelations attributed to the apostle John within a century of Christ's death. [5]

But what is even more important than the attempt to define Christ's exact meaning in the terms of his own temporal and political reference, is to discover what the early church understood him to mean, and in particular the thought of St. Paul, whose ideas were taken by later churchmen as explicitly laying out a christian political policy, if not a philosophy.

Before that problem was fully broached, the more immediate needs of everyday political activity were faced by the first christians and solved in keeping with Christ's words and actions. Peter's announcement "We must obey God rather than men" (Acts 5,29) became a watchword of christian behavior when challenged as to their faith, although the attitude toward civil rulers of the early church was prescribed by Paul in his famous chapter XIII of the epistle to the romans. Even more so, Paul's own behavior vis-à-vis the jewish and roman authorities was exemplary, for he comported himself as a well-instructed roman citizen, occasionally ceding to ill treatment, but on the whole demanding his rights of the governor Festus, and the jailer in Thessalonica. In the end he appealed for justice to Caesar, and spent two years in house arrest in Rome.

It was in the pauline *Weltanschauung* that the church's true political theology was expressed and immediately activated, thus affecting the fortunes of the roman empire and of every nation that has come within the orbit of the christian church ever since.

The pauline doctrine on civil obedience almost smacks of the stoic attitude toward the state and political rule; yet it is in keeping with the best jewish tradition and expresses carefully the consequences of christian belief that "all authority is from God" (Rom 13,1).

---

[5] Cf. P. Boyancé, "Les deux démons personnels," *Rev. Philol.* 59 (1935), 8ff; S.Lyonnet-J.Daniélou, "Demon," *Dict spirit.* 3 (1958), 142-189.

Paul instructs the romans:

> Let every soul be subject to higher powers; for there is no power
> but from God; and those that are, are ordained of God.
> Therefore he that resists the power, resists the ordinance of God.
> And those who resist, purchase to themselves damnation.
> For princes are not a terror to the good work, but to evil. Will
> you then not be afraid of the power? Do that which is good;
> and you shall have praise from the same.
> For he is God's minister to you, for good. But if you do that
> which is evil, fear; for he does not carry the sword in vain. For
> he is God's minister, and avenger to execute wrath upon whoever
> does evil.
> Therefore be subject of necessity, not only from wrath, but also
> for conscience's sake.
> Therefore also you pay tribute. For they are the ministers of God,
> serving unto this purpose.
> Render therefore to all men their due: tribute to whom tribute
> is due; custom, to whom custom; fear to whom fear; honor to
> whom honor.
> Owe no man anything, but to love one another. For he who
> loves his neighbor has fulfiled the law. (Rom 13, 1-8)

While it is evident that this pericope constitutes for all
practical purposes a commentary on Christ's "render unto
Caesar the things that are Caesar's" Paul's purpose was not
immediately evident to some of the church fathers, such as
Jerome and Augustine. But his meaning seems clear enough.
Secular government holds its authority from God and must
be obeyed as a religious obligation. Should one prefer to do
wrong, he has no right to complain if he is punished by the
secular authority whose power has been given explicitly as a
preventative, to keep the prospective wrongdoer from indulg-
ing his folly. What caused embarrassment to some of the
earlier commentators was the fact that the emperor under
whom this assertion was apparently penned was, at least for
many of the early christians, the demon incarnate, Nero.

But Paul made no distinction of persons in regard to the
virtuousness of the ruler in his personal or political activities;
and would probably have responded if asked, "God is the

judge." It should be evident likewise that Paul was writing under the impression that the second coming of Christ was near at hand. Hence the duration of the civil authority's mandate was limited. In any case, the christian is to obey, pay tribute, render honor because of the love of Christ Jesus that is now the essential motivation of his whole being, since he is a "new creature," enjoying his part as a redeemed son of God. For this reason likewise, Paul dissuaded the christian from utilizing the pagan law courts—not that he challenged their legitimacy, but that their services should be superfluous. As time wore on, however, and he realized that the second coming would not take place in his own lifetime, his attitude toward the use of the good things of this world changed slightly; he was willing that the christian should try all things, as he apparently did himself, accepting what is good (I Thes 5,21).

In the pastoral epistles there is a careful and somewhat reluctant attitude in reference to the state. Christians are exhorted to live and work in peace, and they are to pray for and expect that the civil authorities will make such a life possible (I Tm 2,1f.). But christians ask no privileges, and there is no question of their forming a state or of entering into political life. [6]

One of the examples of christian tolerance of a social evil, due it would seem primarily to their immediate expectation of the second coming of Christ, is the problem of slavery. They have a solution: it is the adoption of a pacifistic attitude toward tolerable evils that merely affect their earthly existence (II Thes 2,6-16; Ti 3,1f.; Pt 2,13.47). St. Paul had already assured them that in Christ all men are equal before God in their eschatological grace and calling. "There is neither greek nor barbarian, slave nor freeman" (Gal 3,28). Hence slaves are encouraged not to revolt (I Cor 7,21-24); but on the other hand masters are told that they are to deal with their slaves in justice and equanimity (Rom 14,4). In the end, however,

---

[6] For the problem and bibliography, see J. Blinzler, "Staat," *Lex. Theol. Kirche* 9 (1965), 695-698.

Paul made it plain that there was no obligation to overcome the passing tribulations of this world.

This pauline teaching was evidently a common attitude in the early church as seems clear from its appearance in Colossians (3,22—4,1), Ephesians (6,5-9), I Tm (6,1-2), and Ti (3,9.10), and above all in I Pt (2,18-23). Here the obedience of slaves to their masters is conceived as a religious duty to be discharged with reverence. The author in fact mentions the situation in which slaves must serve harsh masters (2,18), and suggests that, following the footsteps of Christ, they suffer patiently while doing good. [7]

This passage follows the petrine instruction on the manner whereby the christian generally is to treat with the outside world in which, while considering himself a stranger and pilgrim (2,11), he should deal with pagans reverently. Thus when he suffers detraction on the part of evildoers, he may by his good works lead his enemies to glorify God "in the days of his visitation" (2,12). Like Paul, Peter commands subjection to human authority for the sake of the Lord *(dia ton kurion)*— "to the emperor as presiding, to the rulers as sent by him to exact justice *(ekdikesin)* on evildoers." All this is prescribed in accordance with the will of God, so that the ignorance of men may be confuted. The christian as a free man, not hiding behind a veil of malicious libertinism, will act as a true servant of God. Thus he will respect all, love the brotherhood, fear God, and honor the emperor (2,17).

What did almost startle the early commentators, however, was the fact that in Romans, Paul used the words *diakonoi* and *leitourgoi*—both translated in the Vulgate as *ministri*—in speaking of the "authorities as ministers of God." This brought them within the sacral atmosphere that surrounded the idea of the state in ancient thought, and had a distinct bearing on the thinking of the later churchmen as they tried to cope with their politico-religious significance, both while the empire acted as persecutor, presumably under the stimulus of the demons

---

[7] Cf. H. Greeven, *Das Hauptproblem der Sozialethik in der neuen Stoa und in Urchristentum* (Gütersloh, 1935); J. Höffner, *Christentum und Menschenwürde* (Trier, 1947).

as the instrument of satan, or the powers of evil, and after the state became christian and its rulers attempted to control, at least in part, the church's belief and administration.

For besides offering a practical solution for the christian's immediate conduct in dealing with the state, Paul had entered into the far more complex problem of the nature of the kingdom of God and of its opponents in the eschatological order. Paul announced Christ's claim to kingship in the sense of the universal ruler of the world, urging the christian to "confess with his mouth that Jesus is Lord—*kurion Iesoun*" (Rom 10,9). This was in effect a direct challenge to the supreme authority of the civil ruler who claimed to be alone the *kurios* or godlike governor of the roman empire.

Paul frequently speaks clearly of the reign of the Son of God, particularly in the first epistle to the corinthians (I Cor 15,23-28) where, having contrasted the death of all mankind with the return of Christ, he maintains that Christ's reign will be prolonged until the end, when, having overthrown every "principality and virtue and power," he will have handed back his kingdom to God and the Father. This same idea of Christ's kingdom as given to him by the Father is dealt with in Colossians, where it is connected with the redemption "through his blood and the forgiveness of sins" (Col 1,12-14).

The kingdom of God in Paul's thought began with creation; it had its localization on earth with the resurrection of Christ and the sending of the Holy Spirit who, as a sign of the universality of the new kingdom, abolished the separation of nations symbolized by the pentecostal reception of Peter's discourse by the men from diverse lands "each in his own tongue" (Acts 2,8). The church likewise had its inception with the coming of the Spirit on Pentecost. But Christ's kingdom and the church are not fully identical. Christ's reign is over all men, whom he had redeemed once and for all. But the church that Peter revealed by his preaching to "the religious minded men from every nation under the heavens" (Acts 2,5-6) consists immediately of those who have accepted the grace of faith and been baptized "through the one Spirit in one body" (I Cor 12,13). By this baptism they have been incorporated in the

death and resurrection of Christ, that are necessary precon-
ditions of the church (Rom 6,3).

Neither Peter nor Paul thereby excluded the unbaptized
from either salvation or subjection to the kingdom of Christ.
This is part of the great mystery. But they do seem to make
a clear distinction between the kingdom of Christ and the
church as such, though both have the same objective, namely,
overcoming the rulership of "the princes of this world ... who
had they known ... would not have crucified the Lord of Glory"
(I Cor 2,7-8). These princes are not immediately the rulers
of the roman empire under whom Christ had been put to
death, but the preternatural instigators of this crime, who were
constituted in the mystery of divine providence. Christ had
by his death and resurrection broken their power, without,
however, having destroyed it (I Cor 6,3).

The pauline doctrine of the finality of the supernatural
order that projects into the realm of world politics is thus
beyond the comprehension of even the most learned christian;
but it is not to be ignored, since it does throw light on Christ's
own revelations, particularly in his apocalyptic warnings with
regard to the exercise of secular power on a world-wide scale,
and the pervasiveness of the power of evil that will apparently
manifest itself in a gigantic fashion before the end of time
(Mt 29). Paul's slight lifting of the veil of what lies behind
the mystery of evil in the world is given as a reassurance,
however, that its final effectiveness has been broken, even
though it is to play a part in the history of man's salvation. [8]

According to Paul, the christian is a citizen of the heavenly
polis (Phil 1,3.20). The obedience that binds his conscience
to the present authorities is conditioned by the use the civil
ruler makes of the sword of justice; but patience and long-
suffering that is modeled on God's tolerance of these powers
is demanded of the christian. This obedience, in Paul's
thought, is not a meek acceptance or conscientious toleration
of the vagaries of a dictator. It is rather a loyalty toward the
political rulers and an expectation of security in a peaceful life

---

[8] Cf. O. Cullman, "Kingship of Christ," *op. cit.*

and tolerance, as well as freedom of religious difference, in the sphere of private life. Both the Old and New Testaments proclaim that with God, "there is no respect of persons" (Dt 10,17; Mt 2,2.16); this idea has a strict bearing on the order in community life.

In relation to the everyday world of greek culture, Paul showed very little interest. He utilized the familiar happenings as analogies for what takes place in the world of the spirit—the sports arena, military discipline and organization, and an occasional appeal to literary interests, or the philosophies of the day, as in the speech attributed to him at Athens (Acts 12, 22ff.). He does not envision the christian as intimately associated in these affairs, other than in his necessary contact with the civil officials, and occasionally in conflict with the secular religious cults. In general, he views the world as good, since it is God's creation; but the things of the world he tends to consider sinful, and the christian is not to conform himself to them (Rom 12,3). Hence the wisdom of the world is most often vain; its piety and virtue is misdirected. For the christian, charity must proceed from faith, and his liberty can only be guaranteed if he lives consciously as a son of God. In actual fact, the christian should be continually full of hope because he is looking forward to a new age in which the church of Christ will reconstitute all things in Christ.

The Apocalypse, on the other hand, was written in the midst of persecution, and it reflected the terrible judgment on this world that was handed down in the jewish apocalyptic writings wherein the power of satan as the Antichrist is acknowledged as reaching out for full domination of the world in an immediate political as well as preternatural sense. Yet the world is good in itself and salvageable; but the christian *ethos* must be directed against the powers governing this world.

In the Apocalypse there is, therefore, a passionate protest against the totalitarian type of political rule (13 and 14). Authorities who overstep their competence make a mockery of true authority and power. But the Apocalypse does not challenge the right of the political order as such; and it is neither revolutionary nor anarchic; it is rather turned against the persecuting tendencies of the cult of caesar as it was experienced under Domitian (81-96 A.D.). The author understood the necessity of political order without dealing directly with the power of the state or the origin of its rights. But with Paul he believed in the abolition of all earthly politics in the final constitution of the new creation (Ap 21 and 22), when the "King of kings and Lord of Lords" (19,11-16) will have reassumed all power to himself in accord with Christ's claim. [9]

JOHN AND JAMES

Despite vast differences in perspective, there is a certain similarity in the attitudes of John's gospel and Paul's epistles. John sees the eschatological fact as accomplished in the present, although he looks continually to the future for the perfection of that fact (Jn 5,28f.; 6,39f.; I Jn 2,28—3,2). His accentuation falls on the present tense of the *eschaton* or final happening.

The comings and goings of Christ in the gospel narrative are understood as an eschatological accomplishment. In the encounter with Christ, there is a parting between faith and unbelief (Jn 3,18). The ideas that have a futuristic connotation—eternal life, judgment, those days, peace and joy—are stamped with a present-day significance. [10]

With the epistle of James, this eschatological note is combined with an actuality of detail concerning the particularities of daily life that make the author sound more like an Old Testament prophet than a christian moralist. There is no specific acknowledgment of the civic, political rule under which the author excoriates the avarice of the rich and the presumption of the well-to-do merchants. But the bearing on the political life of the christian is unmistakable.

---

[9] Cf. H. Schlier, "Zum Verstandnis der Geschichte nach der Offenbarung des Johannes," *Die Zeit der Kirche* (Freiburg-im-B., 1956), 265-287; L. Cerfaux, J. Cambier, *L'Apocalypse et l'Histoire* (Paris, 1955); B. Rigaux, *Saint Paul. Les épîtres aux Thessaloniciens* (Paris-Gembloux), 195-280.

[10] Cf. A. Corell, *Consummatum Est* (New York, 1959); E. Schneider, in *Studia Evangelica* (TU, Berlin, 1959), 363-381.

Come now, you who say, "today or tomorrow we will go into such and such a town and spend a year there and trade and get gain," whereas you do not know about tomorrow. What is your life? You are a mist that appears for a little time and then vanishes.

Instead you ought to say, "If the Lord wills, we shall live and we shall do this or that." As it is, you boast in your arrogance. All such boasting is evil. Whoever knows what is right to do and fails to do it, for him it is sin.

Come now, you rich, weep and howl for the miseries that are coming upon you. Your riches have rotted, and your garments are moth-eaten. Your gold and silver have rusted, and their rust will be evidence against you, and will eat your flesh like fire. You have laid up treasure for the last days.

Behold, the wages of the laborers, who have mowed your fields, which you kept back by fraud, cry out; and the cries of the harvesters have reached the ears of the Lord of hosts. You have lived on the earth in luxury and in pleasure; you have fattened your hearts in a day of slaughter. You have condemned; you have killed the righteous man; he does not resist you.

Be patient, therefore, brethren, until the coming of the Lord. Behold the farmer waits for the precious fruits of the earth, being patient over it until it receives the early and the late rain. You also be patient. Establish your hearts, for the coming of the Lord is at hand (Jas 4,13—5,8).

THE PRIMITIVE CHURCH

Almost oblivious of this theological wrestling with the inner complications of the salvation of the world, the early church simply refrained from political alignment. The members of the primitive christian church belonged to small communities that gradually divorced themselves from the temple worship and the liturgical life of the synagogue, under the conviction that the second coming of Christ was near at hand. Peter's "we must obey God rather than men" had a dynamic effect; far from flight from the world, it signified rather a determination to turn the world upside down, bringing all men to repentance for their evil doing, and to entrance into the church in immediate anticipation of the return of the redeemer.

On this tack, while their practice of fraternal charity had at first impressed itself upon their pagan neighbors—"see how these christians love one another"—it gradually lost this note of admiration; and the christian failure to conform to the religious patterns of roman civil life became a matter of suspicion that gradually provoked fear and hatred for the christian name. Paul's experiences as a result of the opposition of the jewish leaders to his preaching "Christ crucified, a scandal to the jews..." (I Cor 1,23) indicate the gradual build-up of the opposition until it reached the proportions of persecution.

Luke mentions that it was at Antioch that the followers of Christ first received the name of christians (Acts 11,26). It seems from the knowledge of the early christians evinced by Tacitus and Suetonius, that it was the romans themselves who gave the followers of Christ this name in imitation of the herodians, the followers of Herod, and similar politico-religious groups. The name had a pejorative significance at first, and in the time of the early persecutions, it was sufficient for a christian to admit *eimi christianos*—I am a christian—to be considered a member of a messianic sect in opposition to the roman emperor. This governmental attitude was most probably influenced by the persecution of the christians under Herod Agrippa, which the lucan chronology in Acts (11—12) has evidently misplaced. [11] This makes the notice in Suetonius' biography of Claudian much clearer: "Rome expelled the jews, rioting greatly at the instigation of Chrestus" (*Claud.* 25). It likewise shed light on Tacitus' *quos per flagitia invictos vulgus christianos appellabat; auctor nominis Chrestus*—whom the rabble called christians because of their crimes, Chrestus (Christ) being the cause of this name— (*Annal.* xv.44), where the word christian had a definitely political significance as Reitzenstein rightly observed.

The fact that the judges were apprised that Christ himself had been put to death under a roman governor was all the

---

[11] E. Peterson, "Christianus," *Frükirche, Judentum und Gnosis* (Freiburg, Rome, 1959), 64-87.

more reason for the condemnation of the christians, his followers in the neronian persecution. The crimes—*flagitia*—to which Tacitus has reference were commonplaces of the current political propaganda, in good part as a result of the jewish accusations against the christians. They included primarily debaucheries in the sexual and ritual spheres, as the apologists of the second century made clear by their refutation of these calumnies against the lives of the christians. This is confirmed by Livy, who says that in the neronian persecution it was not so much "for the crime of incendiaries as for the hatred of the human race"—*odium humani generis*—that the christians were put to death. [12]

POST-APOSTOLIC DOCUMENTS

In the documents that immediately follow the New Testament —the so-called Apostolic Fathers—very little attention is given to the outside world and the problems of national or imperial politics. Instead there is discernible an inner preoccupation with the organization and well-being of the *politeuma* or local community. In the *Didache*, or Teaching of the Twelve Apostles, an anonymous document written most probably before the turn of the second century, scholars see an original jewish instruction or *catechesis* that was gradually christianized. It begins with the key principles of the christian life, utilizing the techniques of the Two Ways—the way of life *(zoé)*, and the way of death—predicated on the two great commandments and the negative statement of the golden rule.

> The Way of Life is this: "First, you shall love the God who made you; secondly, your neighbor as yourself. And whatever you do not want done to yourself, do not do to another" (1,2).

What follows is an explanation of the ten commandments under the influence of Christ's Sermon on the Mount. Par-

---

[12] Cf. E. Peterson, "Das Problem des Nationalismus in alten Christentum," *op. cit.*, 51-65.

ticular attention is paid both to avoiding the sins and perversities of the surrounding world, such as pederasty, magic, divinization—not unknown, of course, among the jews—and to practicing the magnanimity preached by Christ, particularly in the matter of hospitality and care for the poor.

What the document shows clearly is that, while taking over the forms of priesthood and government from the synagogue, the process of separating the christian from the jewish community is completed. Christians fast on the fourth and sixth instead of the jewish second and fifth days of the week; they say the Lord's Prayer three times a day instead of the synagogue imprecations (8,1-2). Special instruction is given for the liturgy on the sunday; and the ceremonies of baptism (7,1-4) and the eucharist (9-10) are described in some detail. Finally, an attempt is made to cope with itinerant apostles and teachers whose charismatic gifts have to be scrutinized for authenticity. There is no reference to the civil authorities in this instruction, nor is any consideration given to other communities or the organization of either christian or civil polity. But the document does afford an insight into the christian ethical pattern, and winds up with a warning based on Christ's prophecy regarding the uprisings of wickedness that will foreshadow the great eschatological event of the second coming. [13]

A second document of similar provenience is the *Letter of the Pseudo-Barnabas*, that concentrates explicitly on the anti-jewish polemic of the new christian communities, and maintains that the hebrews of old, for the most part, misinterpreted the Law and the Prophets, blinded by satanic power. The author localizes the new christian dispensation within the perspective of the prophecy of Daniel (Ps. Bar 4,3-6) and he speaks of a new order in the christian society that is, however, a continuation of the unfolding of Israel, properly conceived. He maintains : "For the scripture concerning him [the Lord], relates partly to Israel, and partly to us" in a commentary on Christ's passion (5,2).

---

[13] Cf. T. Klausner, *Florilegium Patristicum* I (Bonn, 1940), 14-30; J. P. Audet, *La Didache* (Paris, Gabalda, 1858), 435-474.

In a modified jewish perspective the writer looks forward to a time when the christians will mutually possess the earth with dominion over "the beasts and fishes and birds of the heavens" (Gn 1,26.28); but this will only come to pass when "we ourselves have been made perfect as heirs of the covenant of the Lord thus exercising authority on the earth (5,19). For we ought to understand that to rule implies governing so that one may give commands for domination."

In connection with the sabbath, Ps-Barnabas exhibits a millenarian attitude. The author speaks of the six days of creation as six thousand years, after which the Lord will come to judge the godless (15,4-5). He condemns the temple and its worship as a physical object "built with hands," whereas the christian life is not connected with an earthly habitation. It is built upon the remission of sins and hope in the name [of Christ], that gave rise to St. Paul's concept of the christian as "created again from the beginning" (16,1-4). Explicit moral teaching is provided in the form of the Two Ways, as in the *Didache*, but under the symbols of "The Way of Light" and "The Way of Darkness" (17 to 20); and formal reference is made to the resurrection and a final recompense as a guarantee that the righteous man will be glorified in the kingdom of God (21,1).

In his final appeal, the author calls upon "those in high positions" to exercise wisdom, understanding, prudence, with a knowledge of God's ordinances. They should serve as good lawgivers to each other and as faithful counselors (21,2-5). But it is evident that he is speaking of community affairs with no reference to the surrounding polity. [14]

The first semblance of a political awareness on the part of the early christians is contained in the *Letter of Clement* sent by the church of God at Rome to the "church of God that sojourns at Corinth." It begins with a veiled reference to the repeated " misfortunes and calamities that have befallen us," without making specific mention of civil persecution. In

---

[14] T. Klausner, *Flor. Patr.* 1 (Bonn, 1940), 31-69; cf. A. Ehrhardt, *Politische Metaphysik* II, 59-62.

recommending peace and concord to the community at Corinth that has been disturbed by rebellion on the part of younger men, the author described the excellent reputation for righteous living of the Corinthian church heretofore, and remarked: "You were adorned by your virtuous citizenship *(politeia)*, and did all things in the fear of the Lord" (2,8). In the course of his persuasive counseling to peace and harmony in the community, he described the order that God had established in the cosmos (20), citing it again in reference to the resurrection (24), and in his disquisition on the "good-workman" (33 and 34).

In describing life in the christian community, Clement compares the order necessary for ecclesiastical harmony to the subordination of the different ranks of soldiers and officers to the generals and the emperor in an army (37,1-4). He likewise uses the mutual aid offered by the parts of the human body to the welfare of the whole as an example to the rich in aiding the poor; and to the strong in assisting the weak (37,5—38,2). Finally, he certifies the authority of the priests or elders as coming from God, from whom the apostles received the gospel through Jesus Christ. The apostles, he wrote, "preached from district to district and from city to city, and appointed their first converts as bishops and deacons of the future believers" (42,1-4).

In reference to the restoration of peace in the community, the author suggests that the discordant elements should consider the example of pagan kings and rulers who followed the counsel of their oracles in times of pestilence, and sacrificed themselves literally for the good of the community. Likewise, many have gone out of their own cities that an end of sedition might be achieved (55,1).

It is in the prayer hymn at the close that the *Epistle* makes direct reference to "concord and peace" through obedience to rulers and governors upon the earth (60,4—61,3) to whom God has given sovereignty *(basileia)* upon the earth. [15]

---

[15] C. Schaefer, *Flor. Patr.* 44 (Bonn, 1941); cf. C. Eggenberger, *Die Quellen der polit. Ethik des I Klemensbriefes* (Zurich, 1951).

While these considerations are minimal in a political sense, they do testify to an awareness in the christian community of the world in which it existed. And this consciousness is present perforce in the seven *Letters of Ignatius of Antioch,* written probably *ca.* 116 in the course of a journey from Syria to Rome that the martyr bishop made as a prisoner on his way to execution. Ignatius neither explains the crime of which he was accused, nor the reason for his execution in Rome; and while he refers to his captors as "wild beasts," it is obvious from the stopovers they made along the way that he was allowed to consort with the christian leaders who came to meet him in Smyrna and Ephesus, and whom he greets in *Letters* to these churches. [16]

The so-called *Second Epistle of Clement* is actually a homily that appears to be of late second century composition. Its theme is simply the inutility of everything outside the christian faith; and the author refers explicitly to the idea of *creatio ex nihilo.* "For he [God] has called us out of nothingness, and desires that we exist out of non-being" (1,8). Hence the christian is to consider his dwelling-place *(paroikia)* in this cosmos as dependent on his doing God's will, and he should have no hesitation in departing this world *(cosmos).* The epistle emphasizes the enmity between God and mammon (1,6), citing Christ's words about the uselessness of gaining the whole world (Mt 16, 26), particularly when the day of judgment is so near (6,2; 16,3). Finally, in the doxology with which the homily closes, Christ is referred to as the savior *(soter)* and ruler *(archegos)* of eternity.

The suffering of the martyrs consequently is as nothing. What avails is the church, pre-existent and now present in the body of Christ. It is a spiritual reality from above, as St. Paul assures us (14,2), and it is truly the image of the Holy Spirit. No one who betrays the church will receive the original justification of the church. There is here a similarity with Ignatius of Antioch who spoke of "nothing visible being good"

[16] K. Lake, *The Apostolic Fathers* (Loeb Cl. Lib., Cambridge, Mass., 1959), 2. 172-277; V. Corwin, *St. Ignatius of Antioch and Christianity in Antioch* (New Haven, 1960).

(Rom 3,2)... "for I will be a true disciple of Christ when the cosmos can no longer see my body" (*Ibid.* 3). [17]

In the *Letter of Polycarp of Smyrna* there are definite political overtones, as when he refers to "God the Father of our Lord Jesus, the *sempiternus pontifex* and Son of God" (12,2), as well as in the admonition: "Pray for all, and pray likewise for the kings and powers and princes, even for those persecuting and hating you and for the enemies of the cross" (12,3). There seems to be a threefold distinction here between christians, pagans, and jews. While Polycarp considers the roman authorities incapable of conversion, and refers to the jews as the explicit enemies of Christ, he would like to see them spared by the "Judge of the living and the dead, whose blood God will apply even to those who do not obey him." [18]

In similar fashion, Melito of Sardis in his *Homily for Easter* describes Christ's grace as strewn throughout the *oikoumene* or the whole world (Ch. 45), so after the fall all men will be saved instead of being tormented by the overlordship of tyranny and evil. For Christ has chained the devil as Moses bested Pharaoh, and has trod down lawlessness *(anomia)*, enabling christians to be brought from "slavery to freedom, from the darkness to light, from death to life, and from tyranny to the kingdom of the heavens." In Christ there is forgiveness of sins, the passage through salvation; he is their Savior, and resurrection, "I, your Lord" (Ch. 103). [19]

In contrast to these testimonies is the work known as the *Pastor Hermas*, at once a witness to the strength and complexity of the roman church toward the middle of the second century, and an allegorizing attempt to explain the church's function in its acknowledgment of the kingdom of God on earth.

When the Pastor Hermas speaks of the church as "the people of God" (*Sim.* 9.18.4), he means the people whom the Son of God and his angel (Michael) had newly constructed out of the old material. The Tower of the Church to which the

---

[17] Cf. A. Ehrhardt, *Polit. Metaphysik* II, 61-62.
[18] K. Lake, *op. cit.*, 282-301; cf. P. Harrison, *Polycarp's Two Epistles* (Cambridge, 1936).
[19] Cf. A. Ehrhardt, *op. cit.*, II, 69-71.

building materials are brought from twelve surrounding hills is his principal simile. There appears to be a double significance here: jewish readers would immediately think of the twelve tribes of Israel, while the pagan convert would have in mind the twelve animals of the zodiac. [20] The tower itself is placed in a cosmological setting, and it has Christ as its door. It is watched over by seven virgins in white, representing the hours of the day and night, and by twelve black-clothed women who symbolize inimical powers. In these circumstances, set beside the waters on a quadrangular fundament, the tower symbolizes the universality of the church that includes the whole of both the Old and New Testaments. It is being built by six angels who have constructed the cosmos (*Vis.* 3.4) with the name of God's Son as its foundation stone (*Sim.* 9.14.5). It contained the four elements of the cosmos in its quadrangular foundations, and stood before the world began, just as it would outlast the destruction of the cosmos in flames and blood (*Vis.* 2.4.1; 4.3,2-5).

Changing images, Hermas uses the parable of two cities as a further explanation of the church which has its true existence as a *polis* in heaven, far from its earthly stopover. Again the gate to this city is Christ.

For Christ is the law or *nomos*, in the form of a tree whose shade is to cover all sections of the heavenly city, and is to be preached until the end of time (*Sim.* 8.3-2). Likewise the Holy Spirit appears in the guise of the church as "the Son of God" (*Sim.* 9.1.i.). Thus the law and the church of God are bound up with the Son and the Holy Spirit. It is not difficult to obey this law. Hence the faithful christians will readily obey Christ, who is the ruler of justice in the community. And eventually the church will replace the roman empire, with Christ as the eternal emperor and his christians living under his governance forever in eternity (*Vis.* 3.9.8).

In contrast, the law of the earthly *polis* is totally different from that of the heavenly kingdom. The terrestrial state deals

---

[20] K. Lake, *Apostolic Fathers* I (Loeb Cl. Lib., Cambridge, Mass., 1957); cf. S. Giet, *Hermas et les Pasteurs* (Paris, PUF, 1963).

with the passing goods of this world. Many christians are tempted to embroil themselves with goods and possessions, forgetting that they have no right to do so, since they belong to another dispensation and must obey another law, even though they are subject to the threats and despoliations of the rule of the earthly *polis*. The christian's true endeavor is to utilize the goods of this world in giving alms. He can thus avoid losing his citizenship in the heavenly Jerusalem. The reality of this latter danger is so great, owing to the laxity of christian life in the roman church, that Hermas considers himself inspired to proclaim a second penance after baptism that thus far was not permitted. Sinful christians were thus exposed to the dominion of the devil who is difficult, bitter, and wild (Mand. 12.4.6).

Hermas thus enlarged on the reference to the two cities in the Apocalypse. He appears to be strongly influenced by the later jewish prophetic literature, apparently by the vision of V Esdras (10,25f.) and by Baruch (4 and 32), but he is not motivated by the hatred engendered among the jews over the destruction of Jerusalem.

Besides the ideological activity of the early theologians, who helped to develop and preserve the integrity of the christian message, it was necessary for the church to maintain its unity amid the dangers of heresy and schism with which the history of the early church was replete. Here the vigilant action of the bishops had to be exercised not merely in individual communities, but in the neighboring regions and throughout the church. This consciousness of being a universal and integrated church was cultivated by frequent inter-church contacts, as the Acts of the Apostles makes clear with the journeyings of St. Paul and his companions, and as the admonition to the seven churches in the Apocalypse attests. It is also indicated in the post-apostolic documents such as the Epistle of Clement of Rome and the Letters of Ignatius of Antioch; and toward the end of the second century, Denis of Corinth is described by Eusebius as sending exhortatory epistles to many of the surrounding churches (*Hist. eccl.* 4.23,2-9).

During the papacy of Pope Victor I (189-99), according to

the testimony of Eusebius, a series of synods were held at Ephesus, in Asia Minor, in Palestine under bishops Theophilus of Caesarea and Narcissus of Jerusalem, in Pontus under bishop Palmas, in Gaul under Irenaeus, in Osrhoene beyond the confines of the empire, and finally in Corinth under bishop Bacyllus.

These synods on a local level seem to have multiplied during the third century, gradually centering on the primary see in each province such as Carthage for North Africa, Alexandria for Egypt, and Rome for Italy. Thus by the third century, the christian religion gradually took on the character of an integrated factor in the life of the empire; and as such, while its activites were tolerated for the most part by the roman authorities, its own character was affected by the necessity of conforming what had begun as a way of life in a hebrew milieu to a more fully acceptable hellenic culture and civilization. This work of adaptation was performed by the greater churchmen of the late second and third centuries from the apologists such as Justin Martyr and Aristides to Clement and Origen of Alexandria, Tertullian, and Hippolytus of Rome.

---

[11] Cf. P. Nautin, *Lettres et écrivains chrétiens des II⁰ et III⁰ siècles* (Paris, 1962).

4

The Persecutions and the Apologists

The religious cult of the emperor had its roots in the oriental
and hellenistic usages that had originally been adopted by
Alexander the Great and his successors. In the great oriental
states, it was the god who ruled the nation as its *basileus* or
emperor. The king therefore possessed divine qualities as the
immediate vicar or representative of the god on earth. He
was considered a son of the gods; hence as a monarch his
despotic power and position was recognized in his title, and
in the court ceremonial and cult of which he was the subject.
A particular expression of the subservience of his people was
expressed in the *proskynesis* or prostration of the individual in
the presence of the king as representative of the divinity. [1]

In their wars and colonization contacts with oriental
monarchy, the hellenistic rulers took note of these divine honors
paid to the oriental kings, and, in the case of Alexander, they
gradually saw the need of accepting such ceremonies paid to
themselves by their oriental subjects. In 42 B.C., Octavian
made reference to the appearance of a comet that had coincided
with the games organized in honor of Julius Caesar after his
death in 44 B.C., and ordered his apotheosis. [2] This gave a
roman foothold to the introduction of the oriental emperor

[1] L. Cerfaux et J. Tondriau, *Le culte des souverains* (Tournai, 1957);
L. Koep, "Kaisertum und Christusbekenntnis in Widerspruch," *Real. Ant.
u. Christ.* 4 (1962), 65-76.
[2] K. Scott, "The Sidus Julium and the Apotheosis of Caesar," *Class.
Philol.* 36 (1941), 257-272.

worship in the west, a custom that had met with considerable resistance heretofore. While this divinization was confined to honoring the deceased emperor, it had significance in regard to his heir. In recognition of this fact, Octavian allowed his coinage to be stamped with the inscription *divi filius*—son of the divine (Caesar). At first this was taken to mean merely a concrete relationship between the reigning ruler and his divinized predecessor. But as the custom continued, this precise significance was lost sight of even in the west; for in the east Augustus had accepted divine honors, apparently in relation to the newly founded cult of the goddess *Roma*. Gradually a cult of the emperor's genius—*tyche*—spread through the empire. His *salus* or welfare, on a scale that included the well-being of the nation, became the object of regular cere-monial supplications in connection with the celebration of the emperor's feast days. People began to take oaths and swear by the emperor's genius or *tyche*, as they had done by the old gods; and this oath-taking assumed a religious significance. [3]

While faith in the reality of the ancient gods and goddesses had gradually decayed, their place was taken by politically-oriented abstractions such as *concordia, pax, victoria, fortuna, justitia, pietas,* and *fides,* and above all by the *dea Roma* as the object of imperial worship. These changes are recorded on the coinage that was so powerful a means of political propa-ganda. Meanwhile, in the literary style of the imperial orations and rescripts, a fulsome type of honorific phraseology likewise reflected this religious atmosphere; and whereas Augustus had not allowed himself to be referred to in the west as *dominus*, Domitian, a hundred years later, took great satisfaction in designating himself as both *dominus et deus*. On the other hand, Decius in the middle of the third century had shown a disincli-nation for these oriental designations, and made a great effort to return to the earlier roman religious ideas by reintroducing the cult of the older gods, and particularly of Jupiter. [4]

The early christians for the most part interpreted Christ's

---

[3] K. Latte, *Römische Religionsgeschichte* (1960), 300-324.

[4] R. Syme, "The Organization of Opinion," *The Roman Revolution* (Oxford, 1952), 459-475.

words "Render to Caesar, what belongs to Caesar" in the sense of political authority and obedience to civil law. But they had likewise considered the "render to God, what is God's" in a strictly religious sense, and therefore as a prohibition to give religious honors to the emperor. This seems clear from the earliest authentic *Acts of the Martyrs*, as well as from the complaints made to the local magistrates by, for example, the men who had utilized the girl with the pythonical spirit cured by St. Paul in Thessalonica. They charged that Paul and Silus "disturb our city, being jews; and preach in a fashion that it is not lawful for us to receive or observe, being romans" (Acts 17,17-22). Similarly in the Apocalypse, the roman emperor is considered as a beast for whom divine honors or the *proskynesis* are demanded (Ap 13,7-15).

Such requirements as part of the political observance of the christians had to be repudiated. As Justin Martyr explained in his *Apologia* (1.13.3), the emperor was not the son of god, nor could he be so honored, since Jesus Christ was truly the Son of God, and as such he was the authentic *basileus* and savior of the world. In the long run, Christ is the only true *kyrios* or lord since he was God. [5]

These notions were a direct challenge to the roman authority, although, like the emperor cult itself, they were oriental in origin, and quite foreign to the latin mentality as such. This is obvious from the attempt made by the magistrate, dealing with the aged bishop Polycarp of Smyrna: "What is so wrong," he asked, "with saying 'The Emperor is Lord' —*kurios kaisar*—and with making an offering and the other requirements in order to save your life?" When they reached the stadium he made another attempt, "Swear by the *tyche* of the emperor; change your attitude and cry out 'Down with the atheists!' " When finally he exhorted: "Swear, and I will free you; deny the Christ!" the old man answered : "I have faithfully served him for 86 years, and he has never done me harm. How can I now blaspheme my king and my savior?" (*Mart. Polycarpi* 8.2).

---

[5] L. Koep, *op. cit.,* 66-70.

In similar fashion, when the scillitan martyrs of Numidia refused to worship the emperor's genius, the proconsul informed them: "We too are religious-minded; and our religion is simple; and we swear by the genius of our lord the emperor, and we supplicate for his welfare which you too must do!" He promised them: "You can be sure of the indulgence of our lord the emperor, if you will only return to your senses." He was thus only more confused when one of the martyrs, Spiratus, told him: "I know nothing of an empire over this world; rather I serve the God whom no man has seen nor can see with his eyes." When threatened with punishment, he replied, "We have no one whom we fear but the Lord, Our God, who is in heaven . . . we give honor to the emperor as emperor; but we have fear only before God" (*Acta scilit. mart.* 1-5).

More than half a century later, the same attitude is expressed in the *Proconsular Acts* of the martyrdom of Cyprian of Carthage. There a distinction seems to stand out between the official religion of the empire and its cultic acts—*caerimoniae romanae*—demanded by way of loyalty to the emperor. The christians rejected this apparent attempt to resolve the difficulty made for them by the more conscientious magistrates. Minucius Felix wrote : "For princes and rulers are portrayed not as great, selected men, which would be proper, but as gods in shameful fashion; and they are given a false adulation; here is where an outstanding man should receive honors [but not adoration], and love should be shown to the more perfect *(optimo)* (*Octav.* 9.5). Origen had likewise rejected all subterfuge : "We cannot swear by the *tyche* of the emperor, just as we cannot swear by other simulated gods. Since, as already mentioned, the *tyche* is only an idea not dissimilar from understanding and distinction, thus we cannot swear by anything that has no true meaning as if it were a god . . . for to swear by the emperor's genius is actually to swear by his demon . . . hence we should rather die than have to swear by an evil and trustless demon." In the end, the christian assertion "*Christianus sum!*" became a challenge to the empire—it was considered tantamount to the crime of treason.

In considering the phenomenon of the persecutions, as

E. Moreau has insisted, there are theological and political as
well as popular and legendary elements intermingled in the
evidence that render the understanding difficult and a final
evaluation all but impossible. [6]

In the gospel reportage to begin with, there are the
warnings attributed to Christ that give persecution a place in
the supernatural plan for divine salvation—a theological
consideration that Tertullian epitomized in the phrase *sanguis
christianorum semen*—the blood of christians is a seed. Christ
had called those blessed who suffered persecution for his name's
sake (Lc 6,22); and he spoke of sending his disciples like sheep
among wolves (cf. Mt 10,17-23; Mc 13,9-13; Lc 21,12-19).
In Acts and the epistles there is almost constant reference to
the blessings visited on the churches through persecution, and
the Apocalypse apostrophizes the fidelity of the martyrs.

Attempts were made, however, to persuade the roman
authorities that there could be a pacific coexistence of christians
and pagans within the empire such as the *Apology of Melito
of Sardis* to Marcus Aurelius, and the *I Apologia* of Justin Martyr
to the emperor. But with Tertullian (*Apol.* 5.4) and Eusebius
of Caesarea (*Hist. eccl.* 4.26,9), the conviction gained acceptance that it was only the terrible emperors, beginning with
Nero and Domitian, who had persecuted the christians, while
the pious rulers had at least tolerated the new religion. This
gave rise to the thesis of, at first, seven, and eventually ten
great persecutions. Despite the protests of St. Augustine (*Civ.
Dei* 18.52) this notion had distorted the political relations of
the early christians with the empire by insinuating that the
principal difficulties were summed up in a duel between the
odious, persecuting emperor and the pious, steadfast martyr.

In his *On the Nature of the Gods*, Cicero had maintained that
no people surpassed the romans in their devotion to religion
(2,8), and the remark was probably justified; but roman
religion was essentially a public cult without a true theology.
During the third and second centuries B.C., the latin peoples
had been naturally drawn to the oriental mystery religions as

---

[6] L. Koep, *op. cit.*, 70-71.

they sought satisfaction for their conscience problems and psychological desires. Earlier outbreaks of religious fanaticism and indulgence in strange rites, following a catastrophe such as a pestilence or famine, troubled the magistrates and caused the passage of laws against vagrant superstitions. Hence, while it professed full religious liberty, roman legislation kept the temples of strange gods outside the *pomerium* of the city. But in 204 B.C., the Great Mother of Ida was established in the temple of Victory and was acknowledged as receiving official cult by being welcomed to a sanctuary on the Palatine in 143 B.C. However, the fanatical processions and extravagant rites connected with this cult were prohibited as unworthy of the dignity or *decorum—to euprepes—*of a roman citizen. In 186 B.C., a public scandal involving the Bacchanales was investigated and some seven thousand were implicated. The importance achieved by this orgiastic religion was attributed to the oriental slaves imported in 209, as well as to the return of the legions of Manlius Victor from the east in 187. The senate finally ordered the suppression of secret societies and the punishment of public immoral conduct; but it did not condemn adhesion to a strange religion as such. In the course of the next century, there were occasional expulsions from Rome of philosophers and propagandists accused of attempting to subvert the *mos maiorum*, the stabilized moral conduct of one's ancestors. This included several banishments of philosophers and itinerant rhetoricians, along with the expulsion from Rome in 139 B.C. of the chaldeans and jews as spreaders of the cult of Sabazios. [7]

The senate had ordered the destruction of the altar to Isis on the Capitolium in 59 B.C.; and after the defeat of Anthony by Octavian, prohibitions against the monster gods of the egyptians were insisted upon. In 33 B.C. astrologers and magicians had been expelled from the city and Tiberius had banished the *mathematici*—soothsayers—in 17 A.D., while the jews and egyptians were excluded by laws in 19 A.D., as

---

[7] J. Moreau, *La Persécution du Christianisme dans l'empire romain* (Paris, 1956).

propagandists of a subversionary syncretism. During the first
century, there were numerous other instances of the preoccupation of the public authorities with cults that led to the
breakdown of public morals. This surveillance was not
directed against these manifestations as religions; but against
their perverse disturbance of the public order, as the jurist
Paulus asserted in his *Sentences*. In general, while new religious
manifestations were subject to great caution, it was with a view
to preventing troubles and agitations among the people—*ex
quibus animi hominum moveantur.* [8]

The emperor Augustus had attempted a thorough reform
of the roman state, appealing in particular to the poets Virgil
and Horace to serve as publicists for a return to the public
piety of the old virtuous romans. Likewise he had come to
the conclusion that the sole means of unifying the great variety
of people and races within the empire, who differed so obviously
in language, religion, and custom, was to institute a public cult
centered on the figure of the emperor. Leeway was given in
the expression of this cult through either the adoration of the
emperor or his genius, or by sacrifice to the gods for his well-
being. Under Tiberius, there is no indication that this cult
was prosecuted as obligatory; but with Caligula, Nero, and
Domitian, there were instances of absolute demands that the
emperors be adored as gods. However, until the reign of
Trajan, there did not seem to be a direct confrontation between
christians and the emperor on this score.

St. Augustine controverted the thesis that the persecution
of the christian religion as such had begun with Nero (*Civ.
Dei* 18.52). In fact, the christians enjoyed the immunities
granted to the jews by Julius Caesar and Augustus that had
continued in force until the great jewish revolts that broke out
in Palestine in A.D. 66, and were put down with the destruction
of the temple of Jerusalem by Titus and Vespasian in 71 A.D.

There had been local difficulties among the jews themselves
in 40 A.D., at Antioch, and in 41 at Alexandria, that were

---

[8] Cf. H. Last, "The Study of the Persecutions," *Jour. Rom. Stud.* 27
(1937), 80-92; "Christenverfolgungen II," *Real. Ant. u. Christ.* 2. 1208-1228.

brought to the attention of the higher roman authorities. However, these do not seem to be the results of the split between the jews and the christian converts. But it does seem that the expulsion of the jews from Rome under Claudius chronicled by Suetonius—*impulsore chresto*—was due to the agitation in the synagogues caused by the preaching of christianity. [9]

After the burning of Rome in 64, Tacitus explicitly accuses Nero of having turned on the christians as scapegoats for the disaster. They were judged guilty of a hatred for the human race—*odium humani generis*—and were put to death in large numbers in the gardens of Nero that served as a circus "for the satisfaction of the cruelty of one man" (Tacitus, *Annales* 15,44). The *Epistle of Clement of Rome* (*ca.* 100 A.D.) warns that it was because of internal "jealousy and envy that this catastrophe had been visited upon the christians—particularly on Peter and Paul and a large number of the elect, including women" (*Epist. Clem.* 6). While the tradition of the persecutions that really begins with Eusebius' *History of the Martyrs* traces an almost continual suppression of the christian faith under Nero, Trajan, Hadrian, and Antoninus Pius, there is no supporting evidence for this supposition. Instead, there are indications of local suppressions, owing to the agitation of the people against christians, such as is evidenced on the part of the statue-makers of Ephesus against St. Paul recounted in Acts (19,21-34). On the other hand, the legends concerning many of the nobility, including Flavia Domitilla, as christian members of the imperial household, do not seem to have a justifiable foundation.

There was, however, another side to this coin. The christians had inherited from the jews the necessity of praying for the emperor and for the well-being of the state. This custom was consecrated by New Testament doctrine, and eventually combined with the notion that the empire had served as a providential linking together of the world hegemony at the time of Christ's birth. The empire was likewise an instrument rendering Christ's command "to teach all

---

[9] J. Moreau, *op. cit.*, 21-28.

nations" possible. This idea formed what has been referred to as an "Augustus theology." [10]

In his own lifetime, Augustus had laid plans for his idealization in history; and this propaganda is reflected in the *Historia Augusta*. With the exception of a few writers such as Tertullian, Prudentius, Augustine, and the Pseudo-Chrysostom, the early christian writers of history had accepted this ideology, connecting it with a providential preparation for the birth of Christ and the spread of the church. Even in the commentary of Hippolytus on Daniel, where the roman empire is unmistakably identified with the last beast of the Apocalypse, no attack is made on Augustus. Instead, the roman census *(apographia)* that was completed by the earthly ruler as a political evaluation of his subjects is compared with their call to faith in Christ (*In Dn* 4,8, 7 to 4.9). In Origen's *Contra Celsum* this juxtaposing of romans and christians, of God and Caesar, is used to assert the subordination of worldly to spiritual rule. Augustus served as a tool for God's providential arrangement. The completion of the universal rule of the *oikumene*, and the proclamation of the *pax romana*, were brought about as prelude to the conversion of the gentiles (*Cont. Cel.* 2.30).

Further in his *Commentary on Luke*, Origen saw the baptism of Christ connected with the reign of Tiberius as a sign of the ecumenical mission of the church (Orig., *In Luc. hom.* 21). Origen had also called the augustan census a *mysterium* whereby the men of all the world were registered in "The Book of Eternal Life," and Jerome translated this as a sacrament (Hier. *Hom. Origen. in Lc.* 11). These two coincidences are given further significance by Ambrose and Jerome. Ambrose, commenting on the 45th Psalm, asserts that the *pax romana* was achieved to enable the apostles to set out on their missionary journeys over the whole world (Amb., *in Ps.* 45 : *PL* 14.11.98); and Jerome simply translated the passages of Origen into latin (*PL* 16.284). But Eusebius himself stated that the accomplishment of Augustus was not brought about without God's

---

[10] I. Opelt, "Augustustheologie und Augustustypologie," *Real. Ant. u. Christ.* 4 (1961), 44-57.

aid: the emperor in his mission of peace served as a road breaker for the christianization of the world; and his achievement of the monarchy was a predisposition for mankind's belief in one God (*Demonst. evang.* 3.32).

In a commentary on the Canticle of Canticles, by Apronius, a syrian or persian, probably of the fifth century, the *pax romana* is further noted as part of the christianizing process. The author cites a fragment from Livy concerned with the subjection of the peoples and the victorious return of the emperor; and maintains that the closing of the gates of the temple of Janus coincided with the epiphany, and was the sign of the start of a new era.

Ambrose had considered the census as indirectly caused by "*Christus censor*" (*Expos. in Lc.* 2.36), and Gregory the Great utilized it as a forerunner for the final judgment of all mankind (*In evang. hom.* 8). But it was Orosius, the spanish historian encouraged by Augustine, who had drawn all these references together. By being part of this providential planning, Christ, on allowing himself to be registered in the census, had thereby recognized the roman people as peculiarly his own. And this concept, epitomized in the observation *Christi gratia preparatum Cæsaris imperium*—by Christ's grace the empire of Caesar was prepared—strongly influenced the legends of the middle ages (Oros., 6.21, 7-19). It was surrounded with a series of prodigies centered on the emperor's triumphal returns to Rome (in A.D., 23, 29, 36, and 44), that were said by Orosius to have accompanied the life of Augustus as a sign of his providential role. [11]

This adaptation of the imperial prowess is in strange contrast to the opposition to that same empire during the ages of the persecutions. But it demonstrates the natural connection between religion and politics all during the early christian era. Nor is it actually strange, since the very idea of politics throughout the ancient world was inconceivable without a religious background. Man's destiny in this world is irre-

---

[11] Orosius, *Historiarum libri* vii : 6.20; cf. E. Peterson, *Der Monotheismus als Politische Problem* (1935), 88-93; A. Alföldi, "Der Einmarsch Octavians in Rom," *Hermes* 86 (1958), 480-496.

trievably connected with his relation to something beyond this world; this is part of an irradicable human psychology, as contemporary events seem likewise to attest.

THE APOLOGISTS

In the course of the second century there had appeared a number of *Apologies* defending the christian way of life and attempting to bridge the difference between christianity and the pagan philosophy, to allay the enmity between the church and the empire. The first such significant effort was apparently made in a lost document known as the *kerygma* or Preaching of Peter that is cited with some frequency in Clement of Alexandria, and that had apparently a double purpose: a refutation of the calumnies spread against the christians, and an exhortation *(logos protrepticos)* to belief in the one true God and in Jesus Christ his Son. [12]

These apologies were written by men of some education who had been converted to the christian philosophy, and had set about both justifying their adherence to the new faith, and demonstrating the truth of christianity as the sole safeguard for the continuance of the civilization and empire of which they were part. Christians had inherited the reproach of being misanthropes (or *amizia*) used against the jews that Tacitus had summed up in the charge of *"hatred of the human race."* They were considered atheists in their refusal to adore the pagan gods, and to participate more particularly in the cult of the emperor. This had led to a series of calumnies, including accusation of ritual murder and incest in their secretive meetings and religious ceremonies.

These accusations, spread among the populace, gave rise to constant suspicion and were apparently encouraged by the jews, who refused to see in christianity the fulfilment of their own messianic prophecies. They led to frequent polemic exchanges, and to a fear of disorders on the part of the civil authorities.

---

[12] M. James, *The Apochryphal New Testament* (Oxford, 1924), 480-496.

During the course of the second and third centuries accordingly, christianity was conditioned in its political thought by the persecutions that affected the new religion in various parts of the roman empire. Writing to the philippians in 50 A.D., Paul had been conscious of the fact that they formed a solid bloc among the local inhabitants; and in a few years the church had spread through the great cities of Greece and on to Rome. By 112 A.D., the *Letter of Pliny the Younger* to Trajan from Amastris in Asia Minor attested to the fact that by the turn of the second century, the new religion was spread among people of all ages and of both sexes in cities, towns, and country places throughout the empire, as well as in Pontus and Bithynia, so that christians were considered a formidable group, capable of causing riots and revolutionary activity—a primary concern of the roman civil government.

What is likewise of interest is that while the fact of being a professed christian was considered a crime, it was not because of allegiance to a god foreign to roman belief. It was rather that, in refusing to participate in the honor given to the emperor and the state gods, they were considered obstinate fanatics who defied the power of the civil authority. Pliny testified to the fact that upon questioning, christian apostates asserted that their religious practice consisted in rising before the sun on fixed days, chanting hymns in alternate choirs to Christ as God, and binding themselves by oath not to commit any crime, neither burglary, nor brigandage, nor adultery. They were obliged likewise to keep faith in a promise, and to restore whatever was entrusted to them. The religious repasts of the christians were innocent of scandal or crime; and Pliny had obtained proof of these facts by torturing two slaves called deaconesses.

Trajan's reply that christians were not to be sought out, but that, when apprehended, they were to be punished for obstinacy, and that anonymous delations were to be repudiated, became the rule for succeeding decades. [13]

---

[13] Cf. E. Peterson, "Christianus," *Frühkirche, Judentum und Gnosis,* (Freiburg, Herder, 1959), 64-87; J. Moreau, *La Persécution...,* 21-64.

While this decision was attacked by the christian apologists from Quadratus to Tertullian as lacking in consistency, it was actually a measure of practical politics, and seemed to be the only possible attitude of a government that was tolerant of all religions so long as they did not prove inimical to the public order. What the apologists repudiated was the charge of gross crimes through which their co-religionists were calumniated by propagandists such as Fronto, Crescens, and Apuleius in the middle of the second century. They had likewise to turn attention to the political significance of the charges of atheism, hatred of the human race, sacrilege, and treason, as well as hostility against the state, that were leveled against them by their more serious critics.

What bothered the local populace among whom the christians lived was their conspiratorial-like attitude in their religious ceremonies, their fraternity that gave rise to suspicions of unnatural crimes, and their refusal to participate in the public religious functions performed for the well-being of the local city and the empire. They thus held the christians responsible for public calamities, such as floods, fire, and famine, reverses in war, and the other evils affecting the common welfare; and they attributed these disasters to the offended gods or demons. Part of this suspicion was enhanced by jewish propaganda, since the jews were considered a *religio licita* by the romans; and although, generally speaking, they were looked upon as potential trouble-makers, it was easy for them to incite the populace, and occasionally the government, against the people they considered apostates to their own religion.

Among the christians themselves, the numerous heretical sects that made their appearance at the turn of the second century were another source of difficulty leading to local and government suspicons.

In answering these various objections, the apologists were greatly influenced by the stoic, cynic, and pythagorean criticism of the pagan gods. These writings furnished them with a sufficiency of argument in deriding the pagan religion, and in pointing out the superstitious character of the greek and roman cults. They turned the stories of the lascivious activities of the pagan gods against their critics; and in countering the denigrations of the christian way of life, they pointed to the purity of the christian moral teaching, based upon a belief in a sole living and all-seeing God, and the splendor of life in Christ. [14]

While the earlier apologists emphasized the uniqueness of the christian attitude toward life—both the author of the *kerygma* of Peter and Aristides had spoken of christians as a "third race" *(triton genos)* between the greeks and jews—later writers such as the author of the *Epistle to Diognetus* and Justin Martyr saw a danger in this tactic, and followed instead the lead of St. Paul, who argued that in Christ there was neither greek nor jew, slave nor free, but that all men belonged in the christian religion. This cosmopolitanism was not exactly new; it had been preached by the stoics of an earlier generation. But with the christians it took on a new vigor, and could be justified to a large extent by the universal character of the christian communities in so many different parts of the empire and even outside the roman aegis.

What the *Epistle to Diognetus* stressed was the fact that the christians had a vital part to play in the empire. They were not to be distinguished from the rest of mankind by speech, country, or customs. They neither founded cities of their own, nor used a peculiar language, nor cultivated an eccentric way of life. They conformed to the customs of the *politeia* where they dwelt, in dress, food, and mode of life. While so doing, they resided in their respective countries, but as aliens; they participated in local activities, but as foreigners. In this, of course, they differed little from a majority of people living in the roman cities who did not possess the citizenship of the empire, reserved for born or naturalized citizens.

The author asserts likewise that the christians married like all others, and begat children; but they did not expose their offspring. Their board they spread for all, but not their beds. While they were poor they enriched many. Although they

---

[14] Cf. A. Ehrhardt, *Polit. Metaphysik* 2. 57-90.

constantly did good, they were penalized as evildoers; but when penalized they rejoiced. The jews made war on them as foreigners, the greeks [romans] persecuted them, and those who hated them were at a loss to explain their hatred.

But what is of most significance: "What the soul is to the body, the christians are to the world" (*Epist. ad Diog.* 5-6.1). This comparison was particularly apt in a society that believed with the stoics that there was a world soul. The pseudo-aristotelian document *De mundo* had taught explicitly that:

> The soul that keeps us alive and lives in our houses and cities reveals itself by its actions: through it, all that governs life has been discovered, ordained, and maintained on plantations and in the cities, in the administration of the states, in technical inventions, in the practice of law, in order in the state... It should be thought of in the same order as God.... (*De mundo* 6, 399b, 14-25). [15]

With the apologist Aristides, this idea became a commonplace: the good things in the world are due to the presence and prayers of the christians; and God exercised mercy in dealing with the world precisely because of the christians, an idea that will be expressed later in the works of Tertullian and Origen.

In the mid-second century, Justin Martyr directed his Apologies to the emperors and to the roman senate, thus attempting to take direct political action. A convert to christianity, he had run the gauntlet of the pagan philosophies, and had travelled from his palestinian birthplace of Nablus (modern Sichem), where his father was a soldier colonist and consequently a roman citizen, all over the roman world in search of truth and a philosophy of life. Hence he took up the defense of the christian religion and community with unflinching courage—what Paul had called *parrhesia*, or using the freedom of the sons of God.

Repelling both the crimes attached to the name of christian and the charges of perversity, Justin accused the roman

---

[15] Cf. H. I. Marrou, *A Diognète* (Paris, Sour. chrét. 33, 1951), 142.

authorities of being agitated by the insane lust and the stimulus of the demons in their persecutory attitudes (1 *Apol.* 5.1). While he acknowledged that the emperors generally strove after philosophy and piety, he accused them of giving way to calumnious traditions, instead of seeking out the truth concerning the christians. In actual fact, Justin maintained the government not only tolerated evil of every kind, but actually attempted to exact taxes and payments from practitioners of perversity whom it should rather have hunted out of the empire (1 *Apol.* 27.1-3).

Describing the moral teaching of Jesus Christ, particularly as it is explained in the Sermon on the Mount (Mt 5—7), Justin insisted that in following the christian way of life, the followers of the master could not but be good citizens of the empire (1 *Apol.* 13-16), and this included paying taxes and tribute in keeping with Christ's admonition to "render to Caesar the things that are Caesar's" (*Ibid.* 17).

He warned the rulers against the snake as the symbol of eternal Rome since it was associated with the cult of a demoness, the *Magna Mater;* and assured them that in the final retribution, they would face the just judgment of God, not as Plato described it before the bar of Minos and Rhadamanthus, but with the possibility of eternal damnation (2 *Apol.* 8.4; 5; 11.1).

Justin solved the problem raised by the skeptics that among different peoples various, even contradictory, values were upheld as virtuous and good, by asserting that such perversity was obviously the achievement of the demons (2 *Apol.* 9.2). At the same time, he expressed positive hope in the possibility of converting the roman empire to true peace in Christ (1 *Apol.* 12.1). This would be achieved by accepting the doctrine of the *logos* who had overcome the power of the demons.

To demonstrate how far this was from absurdity, as an appeal to the sophisticated stoics then ruling the empire, Justin cited the fact that Socrates had obviously made a similar attempt to liberate the polity of his day from demonic subjection (1 *Apol.* 5.31; 2 *Apol.* 7.3). He thus indicated that he was aware of the contemporary discussion of Socrates' role on the part of Plutarch and Apuleius. But this adherence unto death to the truth of the *logos* also characterized even stoic philosophers such as Heraclitus and Musonius (2 *Apol.* 8.4), who, since they had suffered for the truth, were christians before the fact (1 *Apol.* 45.3). All truth, therefore, was involved with the *logos* who had become incarnate for man's sake; and his truth abided not merely in the philosophers and the literate, but was confided likewise to the laborer and the unlearned. For the *logos* is the power of his indescribable Father, and not merely the depository of human wishes.

Justin summed up the idea of conversion to true citizenship:

> "Before we became christians," he declared, "we took pleasure in debauchery; now we rejoice in purity of life. We used to practice magic and sorcery; now we are dedicated to the good, unbegotten God. We used to value above all else money and possessions; now we bring together all that we have and share it with those who are in need. Formerly, we hated and killed one another and, because of a difference in nationality or custom, we refused to admit strangers within our gates. Now since the coming of Christ, we all live in peace. We pray for our enemies and seek to convert those who hate us unjustly, in order that, by living according to the noble precepts of Christ, they may partake with us in the same joyful hope of obtaining reward from God, the Lord of all" (1 *Apol.* 1.14). [16]

Justin's disciple, the syrian philosopher and cynic Tatian, addressed an *Oration to the Greeks* in which he attempted to destroy the ancient cosmology and pagan theology by attacking directly the cosmopolitanism of the second century. He maintained that the demons were created in subjection to the Son of God who ruled over the *oikonomia* of the universe; but that some of them had misused their free will to bring about a split between justice and evildoing. He opposed the idea of fate, and maintained that man's free will was responsible for his wrongdoing. Man had been given God's law *(nomos);* hence when he followed the enticements of the demons he was at

---

[16] Ed. G. Rauschen, *Florilegium Patristicum* 2 : S. Justini apologiae duae (Bonn, 1911), 31; on Justin, see J. Quasten, *Patrology* 1. 196-219.

fault. Astrology was a creation of the demons to mislead men
to believe in fate, and then to acknowledge the divinity of the
evil spirits.

There is no compromise between christianity and the
pagan state in the mind of Tatian; hence there is no value in
any of the accomplishments of the empire. He sees his task as a
thoroughgoing iconoclast, desirous of destroying the philosophy
by which the pagan lived, and thus forcing him to come to the
truth in christianity. He offered no true solution for the political problems of the empire, and in the end tried to interpret the
christian documents in an encratic or severely ascetical sense,
leading to complete withdrawal from the world. To do this
he had to delete whole portions of the gospels and the other
New Testament documents—a tacit admission that he was not
preaching a wholesome or integral christianity. [17]

IRENAEUS

By contrast, Irenaeus of Lyons (d. *ca.* 200) rendered a twofold
service to the christian theology: he gave it a solid foundation
in the scriptures with the church as its deposit and guardian;
and he laid down guide-lines for the understanding and control
of tradition whereby the apostolic succession and therefore the
historical continuity of the church could be recognized. At
the same time he demonstrated from the jewish experience
that an uncontrolled reliance on local developments as part
of the tradition could lead to the excesses and obscurities in
religion that were now evidenced in the gnosticism he had to
combat. When Christ completed the law and the prophets,
he abolished the need for jewish traditions. The new covenant
was contained in the New Testament; its terms and their
extension, with the expansion of the church, needed no secret
traditions such as the gnostics claimed for their understanding.

---

[17] Cf. M. Elze, *Tatien und seine Theologie* (Göttingen, 1960); R. Grant,
"Theophilus of Antioch," *Harv. Theol. Rev.* 40 (1441), 238-241; J. Geffken,
Zwei griesch. Apologeten (Leipzig, 1907), 105-113.

They were evident in the local churches and apostolic succession that he proceeded to describe. [18]

A. Ehrhardt sees in the irenaean insistence on a *natural law* in the regulation of tradition the influence of the development of *naturalis æquitas* in roman law. He maintains that it is no coincidence that Irenaeus seized upon the roman recognition of the power contained in its strong tradition of office, to insist upon the continuity of apostolic power in the bishoprics, and particularly in that of the roman see. [19]

The analogy is striking, and most probably correct. The tradition of explaining and expanding the jewish law resembled a potpourri from which the rabbi or commentator extracted pertinent texts or analogies almost by chance. Roman law was rather like a bamboo tree, growing generation by generation through the re-echoing decisions of officials following precedents, even when there had to be a radical reconsideration of an administrative procedure, or the application of law to a totally new situation. Thus the roman praetor was continually appealing to *naturalis æquitas* when he proclaimed that "the living voice of civil law"—*viva vox iuris civilis*—demanded such a decision; and the Digest of Justinian asserted as a principle of Gaius: *hac parte proconsul naturali æquitate motus*—in this case, the proconsul was motivated by natural equity. The problem was, of course, that equity usually meant what seemed just and proper to the individual roman administrator.

Irenaeus in similar fashion appealed to "the living voice of the church"; and in this, the christian procedure diverged again from the jewish tradition, where neither the high priests nor the magistrates, but rather the rabbinic scholars interpreted the law and set precedents. What Irenaeus meant by the voice of the church was that of the bishops; and he justified this departure from the ways of the synagogue by maintaining that christianity was the church "called from among the gentiles."

---

[18] Cf. G. Wingren, *Man and the Incarnation* (Edinburgh, London, 1959), esp. 65-72; 147-181.
[19] A. Ehrhardt, *Polit. Metaphysik* 2. 93-114.

This tradition in the church was an unwritten norm compared to the doctrine inscribed in the Gospels, Epistles, and Acts, but it was the living voice of the *magnæ civitatis novi testamenti*—the great city of the New Testament (*Adv. haer* III. 2,6; II.58). Hence Irenaeus could insist that it supported a true freedom (IV.9,2): "That legislation is the greater which is given for liberty rather than for servitude"; and, "that brings liberty to those who serve it legitimately with a right and full intention." The parallel to this sentiment is recorded in the statement attributed to Augustus in the *Res gestæ:* "I have vindicated the republic oppressed by the domination of factions" (p. 48, n. 3). [20]

Irenaeus' understanding of the state seems to be synthesized in his description of St. Paul's conversion:

> This is the secret of which Paul says that it was revealed to him in his visitation (before Damascus), namely, that the One who suffered under Pontius Pilate, is the Lord of the World, its caesar and judge (*Adv. haer*. III. 12,9).

Paul had said that as a consequence of his vision of the resurrected Christ before Damascus, he had begun to preach Jesus Christ; to bring to the gentiles the gospel of the forgiveness of sins, so that they could enjoy the inheritance with those who were made holy through faith in Christ, and received liberation from the "power of satan" (Acts 26,18). While this statement had an eschatological significance, Irenaeus pushed it further in his explanation of the fact that it is Christ who is the Lord of all, the *pantocrator*, the king and God referred to by St. Paul, and not the lord *(euergetes)* in whose name Pilate had put Christ to death. He thus gives expression to his reservations about the caesar and the roman state. Pilate in this instance acted with power extended to the state by satan. But the fault lies very much with Pilate himself since he was acting as "the just king who is of priestly rank" and therefore bound to justice, even though he had to use discretion in dealing with

---

[20] Cf. C. Wirzubiski, *Liberty as Political Ideal* (1950); A. Ehrhardt, *op. cit.*, 97-98.

regulatory law, as Christ intimated in the story of king David when the latter ate the bread of the propositions (Mt 12,4).

While the roman state was implicated in Pilate's unjust decisions it is not satan but God who has instituted earthly kingdoms (*Adv. haer.* V. 24,1). Hence as Pilate was exercising authority entrusted to him by God, he had the obligation of investigating the charges leveled against Christ; and acting with full justice. But in the final analysis, the mystery of redemption was involved; and God allowed satan to mislead the roman procurator, involving likewise the jewish high priest and religion as part of this transterrestrial happening. It was Pilate who was literally pardoned by Christ from the cross when he said, "Father forgive, for they know not what they do."

The political doctrine of Irenaeus is primarily a commentary on the claim of satan in the temptation of Christ to be the Lord of the World (Lk 4,6) with a refutation from the book of Proverbs (21,1;8,15). It is likewise influenced by St. Paul's statements on worldly power (Rom 13,1-20), together with Christ's acceptance of the obligation of paying the tribute to Caesar. The immediate implications of these considerations concerning the secular world of everyday politics is not spelled out in those of his works that have been preserved. They are taken into consideration by the next generation of apologists and theologians such as Hippolytus and Tertullian in the west, and Clement of Alexandria and Origen in the east.

5

Alexandria, Rome, Carthage

Of alexandrian christianity, despite the possible information
engendered by localizing there such post-apostolic documents
as the Epistle of Pseudo-Barnabas, nothing is known with
certainty until the sudden appearance of Clement of Alexandria (*ca.* 180 A.D.) with a school of christian philosophy
and his triad of books called the *Protrepticos, Paidagogos,* and
Stromateis. The city itself was the second great metropolis of
the roman empire; and it proved to be Rome's greatest
political problem, since it was continually in danger of uprisings
that threatened roman hegemony in Egypt, and the whole of
the east. Dio of Prusa (*ca.* 100 A.D.) testified to the philosophical opposition to roman rule centered in its university;
and various of the christian *Apologiæ ad græcos* or *Adversus gentes*
seemingly had their origin in its environs.

Alexandria had been the center of Philo Judaeus' successful
attempt to cross the hellenistic philosophy with jewish religious
thought. And the early christian intellectuals naturally followed his lead in attempting to accommodate the teachings of
Plato and the stoics to the doctrines of their religion. At the
same time, their presence in the university proved a challenge
to the pagan philosophies, and men like Aulius Aristides and
Celsus (fl. *ca.* 180) took the trouble to examine the christian
scriptures carefully and to attack the christian way of life
as inimical to both sound philosophy and the state. Both
these opponents of christianity apparently belonged to the

pro-roman party, and this seems to have influenced their attitude toward the new religion, testifying to the opposition it represented in the minds of the local officials as well as the populace.

Of the so-called christian school of Alexandria before Origen, nothing definite is known. [1] A questionable tradition registered by Eusebius of Caesarea links Pantaenus, Clement, Origen, and Heraclas as its successive directors. But it seems more likely that Pantaenus and Clement conducted individual schools of primarily christian philosophy, similar to the neoplatonist courses given by Ammonius Saccas, Basilides, Carpocrates, and eventually Plotinus. Later, at the instance of bishop Demetrius, Origen also organized a catechetical school; but his main attention was centered on what might be termed a christian institute of philosophy as we know from the panegyric of his student Gregory Thaumaturgus, who was to introduce the cappadocian fathers to Origen's writings, once Gregory had returned to his native Asia Minor. [2]

Clement's theological interests were stimulated by the current platonic doctrines and gnostic speculations, as well as by the writings of the stoic Musonius Rufus, and the eclectic jewish philosopher, Philo Judaeus. He accepted the theory, first apparently propagated by Philo and used by Justin Martyr, that what the pagan philosophers had achieved in their search for truth had been purloined from Moses and the Old Testament authors. This legend enabled Clement to pursue his religious and philosophical speculations with impunity as he imitated Philo in reincorporating them into the judeo-christian tradition. He thus became an authentic master of the alexandrian school of christian thought that ran in competition with the emerging platonic current presided over by Ammonius Saccus, and in Origen's generation, by Plotinus and Porphyry, the ex-christian.

---

[1] Eusebius, *Hist. eccl.* 6.6 gives details whose import is not clear; cf. A. v. Harnack, *Geschichte der altk. Literatur* I (Leipzig, 1893), 865ff; A. Méhat, *Étude sur les 'Stromates' de Clément d'Alexandrie* (Paris, 1966).

[2] Cf. Gregory Thaumaturgus, *Address to Origen*, ed. M. Metcalfe (London, SPCK, 1950).

Clement's political philosophy is essentially the product of his ethical teaching. It began with a consideration of the state as in no way supported by divine right. It is rather a consortium, engineered by the demons to deprive man of the fundamental liberty with which he was endowed by his maker, and of which he had been robbed by the incantations of the gods of greek theology, Orpheus, Cadmus, and Dionysius of Mathymna. These demons were responsible for the slavery of death; and as long as people obeyed the tyrannizing demons instead of Christ, the good king, they would be subject to the evils of nature, including political oppression, war, famine, and epidemics, as well as the lack of peace; nor would these evils disappear while human sacrifice and gladiatorial spectacles were indulged in, since these horrors were a continuation of servitude to man's inimical tormentors, the demonic gods. [3]

What was even worse was the attempt on the part of the state to apotheosize the emperors and their favorites, such as Hadrian's playboy Antinous, making a mockery of divinity. Rome had even attempted to divinize mere ideas such as *concordia* and *fortuna* or *tyche*—senselessly erecting temples in their honor, only, apparently, to have the very demons themselves mock them with the burning down of these edifices. It was against the power of these demons that the christian martyrs had won their victories by achieving the true freedom of the sons of God.

Freedom is thus a primary consideration in Clement's political thought, and it naturally should have led him to a revolutionary attitude toward the roman state. But his considerations had little to do with the state as such. He tended to accept the secular authority and its jurisdictional power, making a distinction between the political regime and the powers of darkness that supported them. It is to the latter that the anti-christian laws were to be traced, since it was the interest of the demons to destroy the christian revolutionary doctrine of divinely granted human freedom.

---

[3] Cf. A. Ehrhardt, *Polit. Metaphysik* 2. 182-203.

"Should not Christ," he asks, "assemble his soldiers of peace
through the peace-bringing melody that he had sounded throughout the earth? He has assembled his army unsullied by blood
through his own blood and word, and promised it the kingdom
of heaven.... Hence we are taught not by war but through
peace... and we wield only a peaceful weapon, his Word,
instead of the manifold standards of war." [4]

On the practical plane, Clement accepted the obligation
of obeying the laws, and he favored a positive solution for the
stoic's questions concerning the propriety of marrying and of
having children. Only he asserted that, as part of the local
politeia or political life, christians were not the chattels of the
emperor, but freedmen, redeemed from slavery at the expense
of Christ's passion and death. The fact of the christian's
freedom had been emphasized by Christ when at Capharnaum
he instructed Peter to pay the didrachma or tribute, first
making clear that it was not as subjects of the emperor, but
as foreigners that the tax was being paid (Mt 17,27). In
this connection, Clement considered the christians as a third
genus, created by Christ from the jews and gentiles. He
drew on the biblical typology of Christ, the church, and "the
first man, Adam," as he rearranged Plato's triadic *politeia*, so
that the first age was made up of the greeks, the second, or the
silver age, of the jews, and the third or golden age, of the
christians. [5]

However, Clement's primary interest was in the ethical
value of law, and he justified this by claiming that the scriptures
spoke of three types of law—political, philosophical, and
jewish—that interested him: "The idea of the commandments
is formed in the testament of the Lord; so also are the laws of
the greeks, and the directives of the philosophers." He believed
that punitive law was defensive for the good of citizens; and
he discouraged the idea that it could truly affect an adherence
to the good, by way of correction. Only the early barbarians

---

[4] *Protrepticus* 2.116, 2; cf. *Paed.* 1.99,1; 2.42,3.
[5] *Strom.* 2.140,1; 3.70,1. In his reference to the didrachma of tribute,
Clement seems to be in error; it was a jewish temple tax, not a roman tax.

had followed a morally useful law, since in the greek city-states, lawmaking usually encouraged immorality. [6]

Earlier in their *eunomia* or primitive observance, the greek lawgivers had forbidden luxury; but even the greeks claimed that these legislators were inspired by the divinity. Thus Minos depended on Zeus, Lycurgus on Apollo, and Zaleucus on Athene. Clement summed up the situation with a blunt: "Hence the athenian obeys the laws of Solon; the citizen of Argos, those of Phoroneus; and a spartan, Lycurgus; but a citizen of the kingdom of heaven follows the law of God." [7] But even a roman ruler, when he punishes a criminal with death, "serves as a symbol of the highest judge, Jesus Christ." It is this latter ambivalence that betrays the essentially hellenistic inner convictions of Clement. He was a thorough christian; but his faith operated within a cultural and political system that, despite its anti-christian sentiments, was in his thinking based on principles that were fundamentally reasonable and therefore good.

Good laws were based upon ethical commands. This was an aristotelian observation that pervaded greek political thought; and it was a part of Clement's mental equipment as he distinguished between law and justice. Political justice is a necessary element; thus if the greeks described laws based on justice as good—hence god-given—so must the christian. Besides, the *nomos* or law had as its purpose the hindering of evildoers. By thus delivering them from present evils, it enabled civilized men to live in harmony, and to enjoy the fruits of contemplation. While Clement denied that such virtues as *diké* (justice) and *sophrosiné* (goodness) were personified in the gods, he did not deny that they had transcendent roots. In actual fact, he admitted that in the greek philosophy properly understood, these elements of the good life were based upon divine mandates. But he maintained that this was but another proof that the hellenes stole what they had of truth from the ancient jews, who had received their understanding

---

[6] *Strom.* 6.161,5; 7.119,4.
[7] *Protrep.* 10.108, 4.

through the revelations made by an angel. Moses then became
the personification of the lawgiver, since he was totally
motivated by *Nomos*, and was thus truly a kingly person.

In the end, Clement saw the true *politeia*, or way of life as
revealed in the scriptures, released from all unreality or theory.
This allowed him to identify *nomos* with the *logos*, in whom all
salvation-oriented legislation was rooted. Thus the patriarchs
of old announced the *nomos* for the future generations of Israel
who, as the prophet Jeremiah noted (31,33), should have had
the law written in their hearts. By contact with the jewish
scriptures, even the pagans, or at least the just among them,
could read this law in their own hearts, and were capable of
identifying *nomos* and *logos*. [8]

The knowledge of the *nomos* and the presence of the *logos*
both before and after Moses were the preordained result of
Christ's redemption. But as Plato had also much to say about
the *logos*, a comparison between him and Moses seemed called
for; and Clement began by stating that both were philosophers
in a technical sense: they were searchers after wisdom. But
wisdom was a prerogative of God alone, as Pythagoras among
the pagans, and Paul acknowledged for the christians. Moses
recognized this fact by describing God as speaking with him.
Clement likewise quoted Philo in proof of the fact that Moses
was truly to be considered the *nomos empsychos*—the living law—
thus establishing a kind of mental concordance between the
mosaic and platonic concept of law. [9] In fact, Clement quoted
Numenius as saying that in the end Plato proved to be no
more than an "atticizing Moses" (*Strom.* 1.150,4).

In all these considerations, Clement had in mind the basic
fact of the christian religion. The *nomos* or law must be
identified with the *logos*, and it was recognized as such by
Moses, since the *logos* is the incarnation of the second person
of the Trinity, Jesus Christ, who had been present in the whole
of history, not merely revealing but actually exercising virtue

---

[8] *Strom.* 1.166, 5; R. Tollington, *Clement of Alexandria, a Study in Christian
Liberalism* 2 vols. (London, 1914) cites Gal. 3.24 as Clement's source and
justification; cf. C. Andresen, *Logos und Nomos* (Berlin, 1935).

[9] *Strom.* 2.18,4; 2.100, 1 (quoting Philo).

among mankind (*Paed.* 1.9,4). Christ had taught that the true *nomos* was above all considerations of earthly justice, saying that they were truly "blessed who suffered persecution for justice's sake" (Mt 5,10).

Thus the history of the martyrs was a witness to the presence of the "prince of the dead and the immortal, the Lord and Maker of all good, the true *nomos*, the commandment and eternal *logos*." Pindar the poet had induced the fact that the true *nomos* had to be lord of the mortal and immortal. Hence he would have recognized Christ as the true *nomos* which he was, whether acknowledged as such or not; and the christians who understood this fact became members of the royal house, in Plato's phrase. As the main purpose of an eternal king was to secure man's redemption, Alexander the Great and Augustus had both turned their efforts to this task; and all of Augustus' successors had inherited this idea as the purpose behind roman world domination. But this goal was beyond human achievement. God alone is the savior *(soter)*.

In his description of practical political rule, Clement maintained that a governor must fill his subjects with an admixture of fear and reverence; and this is exactly the attitude of the christian toward God. But Christ led his followers as a general directs an army; he became the master in setting out seed for the peasant; the experienced navigator for the sailor; and the instructor in legal justice for the soldier engaged in police activity (*Protrep.* 10.100,4).

Men should adorn their bodies, the clothes of the soul, in order to honor the Lord of All in his heavenly court, since Christ is the *pambasileus*, or Lord of All, for both greeks and barbarians. All earthly rulers as a consequence are to acknowledge this overlordship and not consider themselves in any way divine. To illustrate this fact, Clement quoted Theocritus, the sophist of Chios, who after the death of Alexander told his followers to cease their anxiety, since "you see that the gods die no more quickly than men" (*Protrep.* 10.91,1).

On the other hand, Christ as truly the eternal king ruled all with the divine *nomos*. Earlier, Clement had suggested a comparison between Alexander the Great and Christ, possibly in reference to the Epistle to the Philippians (2,10.11). But he maintained that in fact the perfect christian, the true gnostic, is above all worldly considerations. "The elect despises all the gold under and above the earth, and all rule from one shore of the ocean to the other, since his whole interest is in the service of the Lord." Thus he fell back on the church as the true *polis* or city; it represents for the christian his true *politeia* or way of life, abstracting from immediate governmental rulership. In this sense, Clement's political doctrine might almost be considered revolutionary (*Strom.* 1.18,4).

Within the church he found two classes of christians —somewhat similar to the classes in Plato's republic—the run-of-the-mill christian and the true gnostic. The distinction was a matter of spiritual achievement or quality, for both lived side by side in friendship, employing the axiom of Pythagoras: "Friends have everything in common." God certainly was the same for both; and there should be no difference between rich and poor, for the rich had no right to luxury, but should share their goods as things entrusted to them by God. Certainly men who had received so much from God should naturally, and in accord with his command for justice's sake, share with their fellowmen. Likewise christians conscious of having been redeemed by Christ from satan's tyranny should show themselves as upright men before their slaves.

Actually, Clement regarded slavery as totally unjustifiable, since St. Paul had written that in Christ there was neither slave nor free, greek nor jew. If all men were properly instructed there should be no need for having slaves branded. But at least christians should treat their slaves as free men: "As God, if your eye is aright, is the same for all, both lord and slave." In the final analysis, he accepted slavery, but with the caution that slaves should not be exposed to the vices punishable by pain of death among freemen. Origen, the man who is considered his successor, as a master in the school of Alexandria, would do likewise.

However, neither man gave the institution the sociological consideration that would have led to its repudiation by the christian church. This is a phenomenon all but impossible of comprehension in the modern world. But in actual fact it was only the stoics who of set purpose worked for the alleviation of the slaves' condition, and its abolishment as an institution. In this regard they were not considered so much revolutionaries, as totally out of touch with the realities of the social and economic world in which they lived. While the christians also had a doctrine that demanded a total change of ideology, they applied it to the problem of slavery, but in a spiritual and non-earthly sense. [10]

ORIGEN

Origen's personality represents a paradox. In his ordinary sermons he addressed the common faithful and gave them the benefit of a simple evangelical spirituality sparked by a mystical tonality that urged them to strive for moral perfection by avoiding worldly contamination on an everyday level. He is thus, in Jaeger's phrase, the precursor of monasticism. At the same time, however, in his learned works such as the *Periarchon* or First Principles, in his *Against Celsus*, and in his commentaries on the gospels of Matthew and John, he reflected the movement that began with Philo in the early first century A.D., and that continued through Basil and Gregory of Nyssa to form the byzantine tradition with Denis the Aeropagate and John Damascene. It was a successful attempt to combine the insights of greek philosophy with the revelations of divine reality made in the Old and New Testament, thus giving rise to an authentic christian gnosis. [11]

St. Paul himself drew a distinction between the simple faith or *pistis* of the ordinary believer, and the more complicated explanations of faith required of the theologian. And while it can be asserted that Christ apparently favored the first of these two approaches to religion since, generally speaking, he confined his preaching to the simple people of the city and

[10] A. Ehrhardt, *Polit. Metaphysik* 2. 193-194.
[11] *Ibid.*, 204-227. The literature on Origen is enormous; cf. H. Musurillo, "The Recent Revival of Origen Studies," *Theol. Stud.* 24 (1963), 250-263.

countryside, the gospel account of his actual deeds and utterances reflects the mystery-laden prophetic doctrine of the Old Testament, combined with his claim to be the Son of Man who entered into the world to achieve mankind's redemption.

Faced with the implications of Christ's teaching, once it was disseminated in the world of learning in the second and third centuries, and met with the competition of the esoteric explanation of the cosmic process, as well as of man's destiny provided by the oriental mystery religions in particular, Origen followed the lead of Clement of Alexandria and the apologists of the second century. He set out to give to christianity that substantial intellectual coherence that was required, if it were to appeal to the greek mind. He said this explicitly in his preface to the *Periarchon*, where he distinguished between the valid data of the faith as synthesized in the creed and the commandments, and the conclusions of theological speculation to which he felt himself impelled by the nature of his own genius. This distinction between faith and theology has been a constant in the church's tradition; though in more recent times a confusion concerning the nature of the church's magisterium, and a legalistic approach to the interpretation of the binding force of papal utterances, has tended to confuse the two.

Origen's primary concern with politics was provoked by the attack on christianity provided by the *alethes logos* or True Doctrine of Celsus written apparently some fifty years earlier. [12] Celsus was evidently a protagonist of roman rule and an intelligent scholar who had read the christian scriptures and apologists, particularly Justin Martyr. His attack was thus weighty and influential. He maintained that Christ, at least as portrayed by his disciples, was a revolutionary figure who like many another fanatic in a time of political troubles has used the opportunity to proclaim himself as one sent by God, if not actually the son of God. He was likewise a visionary who had promised the impossible such as the forgiveness of sins, and a personal destiny of the individual in the bosom of God.

---

[12] Cf. H. Chadwick, *Origen Contra Celsum* (Cambridge, 1953), ix-xxix.

Celsus further declared the christians were not consistent. In their opposition to the roman government, they had no right to complain at the fact of persecution. With Paul they should rather be saying "I am crucified to the world, and it to me."

Celsus maintained that the roman empire was grounded on the will of the gods; and that, as Homer had asserted, as a kingdom it was an image of heavenly monarchy (*Contra Cel.* 7.68; 8,67). Everything that existed was good, since it was kept in being by the will of the gods. Whoever resisted the roman state, therefore, was guilty of treason to both the emperor and the gods.

In setting about his reply, Origen seized upon Celsus' citation of Pindar: "The *nomos* or law is king"; and challenged the validity of roman rule by demonstrating its opposition as law to true justice. Thus he introduced the fact that on the earth there were actually two laws striving one against the other: that of sin with its chaotic tendencies; and that of God that tends to virtue. To cite a law as good it was not sufficient to prove it was traditional or patriotic. The christian was willing to admit that many of the laws of Solon, Lycurgus, or Seleucus were just; but this was due not merely to the fact that they were laws. It was because they represented right reason in keeping with God's commands. But the imperial persecutions of christians were based upon unjust laws, and it was a proof of God's protecting might that despite them the christian religion continued to flourish.

In actual fact, the imperial laws were not the handiwork of the emperors; they were rather the result of demonic interference in human affairs, and represented the evildoings of men who served the army of satan. This could be seen in the folly of a judge who rejoiced when a christian apostatized under torture, since this was a mere instance of physical weakness. No christian in his right senses could be made to adore the image of an emperor or swear by his *tyche* or genius. The constancy of the martyrs, however, should not be taken as a sign of their own virtue or strength; rather was it a proof of the extension in the world of God's goodness through the redemption in Christ's sufferings and death. The crucial point to be realized here was that Christ's commandments were obeyed by his followers not from the fear of the sword that confronted the emperors' subjects, but through conviction and love.

Christ as king of the cosmos was the image of God's *nomos* or law; and the foundation of his earthly reign had been laid during the governance of Augustus Caesar. While Christ might be considered a revolutionary *archegetes*, his doctrine did not lead to the overthrow of earthly rulers, but to true peace in the heavenly *politeuma*, the church. Christians were not anarchists, but they simply could not prefer any worldly ruler to their true king, Christ; otherwise they would be forced to obey the law of sin.

God was the lord of the christian's *polis*, and the church his true fatherland. But in fact, all mankind belonged within this kingdom of God, both civilized and uncivilized. Earthly rulers had their power from God as would soon be seen when, on the conversion of all mankind, the service of the demons would cease, and the law of Christ take over. Until then, the pagans were under the guidance of the angels of the nations whose powers God has assigned to them after the dispersal of tongues upon the destruction of the tower of Babel.

Turning to the individual, and applying his threefold exegesis—body, soul, and spirit leading to the historical, moral, and spiritual sense—of the Scriptures, Origen saw in the soul of the christian a city of God (*Comm. in Ps.* 45.4). He comments in this wise on Christ's saying "The kingdom of God is within you" (Lk 12,21). Relying on the doctrine of the pre-existence of the soul, Origen maintained that the soul reflected the kingdom of heaven. Cast out because of original sin, the soul of the perfect christian, the true gnostic, lived in peace and obedience, achieving *eunomia* or lawfulness as did a properly governed city. Guided by Christ, at once the *Logos* and *Nomos*, it enjoyed an authentic liberty since on its own recognition and strength, it fulfiled the law of God. After death, consequently, the soul would no longer be subject to law since it would be united to the *Logos*. Thus as the christian prayed regularly "Give us this day our daily bread," he was requesting

God to maintain Christ as the lord of his soul. The simpler christian could not disengage himself completely from the temptations of the world, and lived in turbulence because of sin and shame. But as he made progress toward justice under God's helping grace, he could prepare himself for his destiny in the heavenly Jerusalem, the city of the saints.

In dealing with the cosmos or the universe, Origen is again influenced by the neoplatonic considerations that he utilized in discussing the nature of the soul as a political entity. In its vast structure, the universe is like the body, each part rendering service to the whole; and over the universe Christ reigns, since he is the lord of all creation. It is Christ's desire to serve as the soul of each christian in his church. Consequently the christian is to listen only to the words of God's *logos*. Should he pay attention to other views such as those of the heretics Basilides, or Valentinian, he will befoul himself. Thus he described the christian imitation of Christ as the *"politeia* of the Gospel," that served as the new testament or covenant between Christ and his followers (*Or. ad Mart.* 12; *Comm. in Joh.* 10.104).

He discussed the church as a political organism, and maintained that while it is in the world, it is not part of the world, but is rather a reflection of the kingdom of heaven that can be seen in the soul of the true gnostic (*De prin.* 1.6.2). It lives in the house of the scriptures; its borders are the chain of the apostolic succession and tradition (*Hom. in Ezech.* 2.2). The bride of Christ, the church, is the pattern of chastity for the christian virgin; and Christ and the church, as bride and bridegroom, are the Light of the World, comparable to the sun and the moon (*Hom. in Gen.* 10.1; *Comm. Cant.* I). [13]

As their head Christ holds together in communion all the individual churches scattered through the empire and beyond it (*Com. Mt* 13.24). He had founded the church on earth through his activity; and when the emperor Augustus registered all mankind in his census, Christ's participation had elevated this list to a ready-made census for the

---

[13] H. Crouzel, *Virginité et Mariage selon Origène* (Paris, 1963).

kingdom of heaven (*Com. Jo.* 19.136; *Ps.* 47.1). As every christian is a member of the body of Christ, bishops through their function as judges become the eyes of the church (*Com. Rom.* 1.7; 2.11; *Hom. Jos.* 7.6). Thus they have a definite relationship to the political life of the empire as well as of the church; and their voice should be heard, and not muffled by threats of persecution and suppression.

In describing the immediate relationship of the christian *ecclesia* or church to the *ecclesia* or assembly of the people of Athens, Origen asserted that the members of the former were steadfast and peace-loving; whereas the pagans among the athenians are full of discord and strife. He says the same of Corinth and Alexandria; and comments that a sociological examination of the facts in the lives of christians and pagans dwelling side by side in two intermixed communities should lead to wonderment at the ability of the christian leaders to bring about such a marvel. The same he insists must be said for a comparison made between the counsel or college of the christian presbyters and the *boulé* or senate of the city. In the one, there is peace-seeking cooperation; in the other, rivalry and hatred. Finally, there is simply no similarity between the encouragement to virtue given by the bishop of a christian community, and the rude insistence upon a mere semblance of public order delivered by the magistrates (*Contra Cel.* 3.30). Later in the same chapter, he lists the benefits the empire receives from the *ecclesia Dei* despite the fact that christians refuse to bear arms for the *civitas mundi*. They educate their fellow citizens and teach them to honor the God of the universe and thus preserve the pagan state from the malign activities of the demonic forces.

Celsus maintained that even granting their adherence to monotheism, it was a false interpretation of Christ's saying "No man can serve two masters" (Mt 6,24) that had caused the christians to refuse service to the state, and that often made them the occasion for sedition among both pious roman citizens and the diverse religious peoples tolerated by the roman empire. He thus suggested that christians cast off their prejudice against the state gods, and join in the government of the worldly city as a realistic sign of virtue. Origen countered this argument by insisting that true patriotic piety could only be found in the city of God. It is not because they desired to escape the burden of daily life that christians refrained from public office, but because they felt compelled to reserve themselves for the liturgy or service of God in the church (*Contra Cel.* 8.75).

Using the example of the jews, whose adherence to mono- theism was as strong as that of the christians, and who yet acknowledged the supreme overlordship of the emperor, Celsus suggested that the christians turn reasonable and have their religion recognized as licit by the state. Origen in reply pointed to the obvious fact that the jews did not proclaim an individual as their lord to whom alone they could give final allegiance. Their messiah, they wrongly maintained, was yet to come; hence they could recognize the emperor as a worldly *kyrios* or lord. But the christian had no Lord but Christ.

In his commentary on Romans, Origen summed up his political creed. He distinguished between *nous* or mind and the *psyche* or soul as he enlarged on Paul's admonition "Let every soul be subject to the higher powers" (Rom 13,1), and maintained that Paul was obviously concerned with those christians who had not achieved a union of spirit with God. They were still involved in worldly affairs. Hence, acting in the realm of the soul, they were subject to the state's authority. Christ himself had sanctioned this obedience when he said, "Render unto Caesar the things that are Caesar's" (Mt 22,21); but Peter and John, by proclaiming "Silver and gold have I none" (Acts 3,6), demonstrated the position of the perfect christian who was without ties to worldly affairs, and thus no longer subject to the power of the civil authorities.

He thus takes up the problem of the persecuting state based on Paul's "There is no authority but from God" (Rom 13,1). While the gospel message also said that power is given to rulers "for vengeance on evildoers" (I Pt 2,14), it is obvious that there is a difference between the proper use and the abuse of authority. Those rulers therefore who misuse their power in persecution of the just will be subject to God's avenging judgment. But meanwhile they are not to be resisted when they command obedience to just ordinances.

In pursuing the pauline statement that the judges of this world are the ministers *(leiturgoi)* of God, Origen argued that the church in its rules dealt only with matters of its own discipline and order. He cites the example of the so-called "apostolic decree" in Acts, where the apostles charged christians to "abstain from things sacrificed to idols, and from blood, and from things strangled, and from fornication" (15,23-29).

"Notice how here," Origen declares, "the method of the Holy Spirit is exemplified in the making of regulations. There are many other crimes that are punished by the laws of this world; hence it would have been superfluous that divine law should now prohibit acts already punishable by human law. The [apostolic] decree only touched on those acts concerning which human law had no pronouncement. They are seen then to be properly the propriety of religion. Thus it is clear that the judges in this world execute most of God's law. For God's law determined that all the offenses subject to punishment by his will should be punished by a judge in this world, and not by the heads and leaders of the church. Paul, being conscious of this fact, correctly calls him "minister of God, and an avenger to whoever commits evil." (*Comm. rom.* 9.26-28).

Origen today would be an advocate of a pluralist concept of society and acknowledge the policy of ecclesiastical abstention from interference with governmental laws that are regulatory of the facts of present conditions. For him it is obvious that sanctity or morality cannot be legislated, particularly not by the state. It is quite certain, however, that his almost contemporary, Tertullian, would have held a severely different point of view; yet despite minor aberrations in the practical order, both men vigorously represented the prosecution of the church's doctrine in the realm of politics.

HIPPOLYTUS OF ROME

The priest Hippolytus, who conducted a school in Rome at the beginning of the second century, was a forthright critic of laxity in the church under Pope Zephyrinus and the papal counselor Callistus. When the latter was elected pope, Hippolytus started his own church as the first anti-pope; but in the salt mines of Sardinia, he was reconciled with Callistus and died a martyr in 235.[14] By way of defining the church, he asked :

> What is the church? It is the saintly community of men who live in justice. For the present harmony that leads to the communion of the saints is the church, the spiritual house of God, planted in Christ toward the east (i.e. paradise: Gen 2,8), in which are found diverse trees of all kinds; the generations of the patriarchs... the choir of apostles... the martyrs... the vocation of the virgin... the choir of teachers, and the orders of bishops, priests and levites (*Comm. in Dan.* 1.1,7).

The juridical character of Hippolytus' apostolic tradition appears clearly from this schematization. In his definition, the church consists first of the clergy, then the laity, and finally the liturgy or service of God. This differentiation of the rulers, the governed, and their activity gave the church the character of a political corporation.

The hierarchy was distinguished by a higher and lower clergy separated by episcopal ordination that gave its possessor as the *princeps sacerdotum* his monarchical rule. He it was who chose and ordained priests and deacons. But the bishop was elected by the community who at the beginning of his consecration signified their consent through an acclamation. [15]

Apparently, the schisms of the third century were due to the growing interference of the priests in influencing the selection of the bishops. Hippolytus attested to the reception of the spirit in the consecration rites that gave the bishop the power of transferring this spiritual force through the laying on

----

[14] A. Ehrhardt, *op. cit.*, 2. 115-131; K. Neuman, *Hippolyt von Rom* (Leipzig, 1902); A. D'Áles, *La théologie de s. Hippolyte* (2nd ed. Paris, 1929); G. Bardy-M. Lefèvre, *Hippolyte, Commentaire sur Daniel* (Paris, Sour. chrét. 14, 1947).

[15] B. Botte, *Traditio Apostolica*. La tradition apostolique de S. Hippolyte (Münster, 1963).

of hands. While the priest likewise received spiritual power through this process, he could not in turn confer it on another; and the deacon evidently did not receive this power, but was rather selected as the personal assistant of the bishop. [16]

In describing the laity, Hippolytus distinguished between the freeman and the slave, the married and the unmarried; and he gave a list of occupations forbidden to the christians. A schoolmaster must not continue as such if he could find another occupation. Soldiers were forbidden to take an oath, and sculptors to make images of the gods. Military and civil officials, because of the loyalty they had to give to the state, had either to renounce their office, or leave the church. In Hippolytus' thought, there was thus a conviction that the imperial regime was governed by a demoniac power. [17]

He compared the church to a ship of the faithful, whose ports were the individual communities. But the ocean on which it sailed was the heartless empire out of which the four beasts of Daniel's prophecy arose (7,17). The kingdoms of this world were the possession of the satanic might, and in the end, they were subsumed in the roman empire, that served as the fourth of the great states in Daniel's apocalyptic description of Nebuchadnezzar's dream. Rome differed from the other kingdoms insofar as it had enslaved all other nations and would not be followed by a fifth kingdom. [18] It would be divided into ten democracies over which the Antichrist would reign; and after that Christ's kingdom would be founded on the earth (*Comm. Dan.* 4.10,2).

Hippolytus does not look upon the church as such, but rather on the christian way of life as the eventual conqueror of the state. In this he is dependent upon Irenaeus. He saw the fulness of the christian party as a goad to Satan, who took his revenge by means of the persecutions. Hence he attempted to destroy the christian life of prayer that could institute a full *pax romana* on earth. Christians had therefore to distinguish

---

[16] Cf. J. Colson, *L'épiscopat catholique* (Paris, Unam Sanctam, 1963).

[17] *Apost. trad.* 16.11; 17-19; cf. Tert., *De coronoa* 11.23.

[18] *Comm. in Dan.* 2-4; cf. K. Neumann, *Hippolyt v. Rom*, 32ff; E. Peterson, *Theologische Traktate* (Munich, 1951), 112ff.

in the laws of the empire between those that served the common good, which they were to obey with care, and those opposed to christianity, that they had to resist unto death. It seems thus that they were to understand Paul's instruction in Romans XIII. Hippolytus used the word *politeia* for the christian way of life and spoke of it as "a well-managed law-fulness" (*nomothesia: Philos.* 8.20; 9.14,1). In contrast to this city of God composed of the saints, the roman state was the new city of satan; but this notion had to be seen in an eschatological setting, as Augustine was to make clear. [19]

As his purpose in composing this *Commentary on Daniel* had been directed toward offsetting the tendency of simpler souls to seek immediate deliverance in the second coming of Christ—he described two bishops who had led their communities into the wilderness, expecting the immediate return of the Savior—Hippolytus had maintained that christians could afford to await in patience the designs of providence, since they had Christ already in the church. Toward the evils of the empire they could adopt a double attitude, as he made clear in his elucidation of Paul's observations regarding obedience to authority. Christians were not to pray for the end of time; but rather that the days of the Antichrist be not visited on them. As the heavenly kingdom awaited all who died in truth, the christian should rather look to God and find release from the passions, sorrow, and sickness of this life in his Son, Jesus Christ. Christ as the conqueror in his agony will crown all those who have fought bravely under his banner, as St. Paul assured the corinthians (I Cor 4,9: *De antichr.* 49).

In his commentary on Daniel, Hippolytus departed from the pauline exhortation to obey the constituted authority. Despite the fact that he was writing a popular treatise to waylay a current of eschatologism, he displayed an incontinent hatred for the roman empire, "the beast that dominates in our time." He denied its unity, and claimed it was a mélange of all the tongues and races of mankind forced into being by unjust recruitment. He maintained that Christ was born in the

---

[19] A. D'Áles, *La théologie de S. Hippolyte*, 175.

forty-second year of Caesar Augustus, since he intended to gather the men of all nations together to make one christian people of them through the preaching of the apostles. He asserted, however, that Satan took advantage of this fact and turned over the hegemony of the world to the romans (*Comm. Dan.* 4.8-9). While God, nevertheless, utilized the roman empire to delay the coming of the Antichrist, it must still be recognized as the fourth beast of Daniel's prophecy. [20]

TERTULLIAN

Tertullian is the first christian author who seemed to realize fully that the roman empire had passed its heyday. He boasted that the name of Christ had broken the barriers of the roman hegemony and was everywhere King, Lord, and God, whereas the roman legions were hard pressed to preserve the frontiers of a far-flung but beleaguered empire (*Adv. nat.* 7). He admitted that as ruler of the ordered roman world, the emperor was a "man second only to God"; but he could not be the object of the christians' adoration. The christian should, however, pray constantly for the emperor as serving God's purpose in holding off the *katechon*, the last day, when the Antichrist would appear in Tertullian's ominous understanding of St. Paul's teaching in II Thessalonians (*Apol.* 32.1). [21]

Tertullian repeated the Apocalypse's observations concerning the succession of world kingdoms (*Apol.* 32) to indicate that the roman empire was not to stand for ever. This was traditional belief, and goes back at least to Irenaeus (*Adv. haer.* 24,1) and Theophilus (*Ad autol.* I.11).

In his general teaching, Tertullian advised obedience to the civil rulers, "but within the limits of our [christian] discipline, so that we break off sharply from idolatry" (*Ad. idol.* 15). He interpreted the Epistle to the Romans XIII in a fully

---

[20] A. Ehrhardt, *op. cit.*, 130-133.
[21] For the text and bibliography of Tertullian, see *Corpus Christianorum Tertulliani Opera I and II* (Brepols, 1954). For political theology, cf. E. Peterson, "Das Monotheismus" *Theologische Traktate* (Munich, 1951), 64-80; A. Ehrhardt, *op. cit.*, 134-158.

orthodox manner (*Scorp.* 14).[22] Nevertheless, he had no love for the roman state "wherein the demons celebrate the sabbath (*Ad spect.* 7) and destroy the body, though they cannot kill the soul," as he insisted quoting the gospel of Matthew (10,28). In the end he cautioned christians to remain aloof from political entanglements: "Be warned! All the powers and dignities of the world are not only alien but inimical to God" (*Ad idol.* 18).

In contrast, christians are God's coinage, stamped with the image of their Lord (*Cont. Marc.* 4.38); and while this world is a prison, martyrdom is the door through which the perfected christian passes to God's eternal freedom. In belittling second marriages, Tertullian asked whether it was really love that would cause a couple to bring more christians into the world so as to serve as objects of pleasure for those who shout "Christians to the lions!"

The world in his opinion was rushing to its end, since justice had long ago deserted it and indecency prevailed. And there was no one who could prevent the debacle clearly foreshadowed by the signs of the times. Hence christians had no business attending the pagan circus and theatre, since the tremendous spectacle at the end of the world was so near at hand (*De spect.* 30). Tertullian's scorn is vented on the rulers of the world, the philosophers and poets, whom he depicts in dantesque colors receiving their just deserts in hell; but this is merely the prelude to the millenium, the thousand years in which the just will reign in the heavenly Jerusalem that St. Paul had called the mother and the *politeuma* of christians (*Adv. Marc.* 3.24).

Despite his lawyer's ability to size up situations, and the service he performed in enlarging the vocabulary of the latin church, introducing such terms as law and rights into current ecclesiastical usage, Tertullian did not offer a solution for the church's organizational difficulties. Nor did he apply his juridical concepts of divine law that so affected western ethical and moral thought down through the centuries, to a discussion

---

[22] Cf. J. Waszink, "Tertulliana," *Mnemenosyne* 3 (1935-1936), 165-174.

of the ends of the state or the virtues of citizens in bringing about concord in the empire. His attitude is strictly deprecatory: the gods are demons who control the state; and the christian's business is to have nothing to do with them. This conviction haunts his doctrine of the redemption, where he pictures Christ buying back mankind, paying a debt to the devil. [23] And this notion likewise can be found behind much of the later western thought as it wrestles with the ontological foundations of man's salvation.

CYPRIAN

A half century after Tertullian's defection to montanism, the convert, Cyprian of Carthage, a lawyer also, but of much gentler stripe, set about that task as bishop of Carthage, though he was martyred in 258 A.D. Rome lacked a figure of his stature, the christian community and the pagan having been grievously afflicted by the decian and valerian persecutions. The empire itself was passing through a period of horrible upset, with interior rebellion rife among the legions, pestilence and famine in the land, and barbarians storming its borders. [24]

In his tract *On Idols*, Cyprian follows an historical evolution of the great kingdoms—assyrians, egyptians, greeks—that differed considerably from that of Hippolytus or of Tertullian. He felt that the Antichrist was already on hand (*Ad idola* 11). Calling himself "a philosopher of deeds rather than words," Cyprian followed the allegorical symbols for the church that he found in the works of his predecessors. But he prized most the idea that the church was at once "the bride of Christ" and the "mother of the faithful" (*De orat.* 31; *Epist.* 59.1,2). Hence, while the christian had God for his father, he had the church for his mother (*Epist.* 74.7,2). It was Cyprian's iron determination and affectionate zeal alone that

---

[23] J. Rivière, *Le dogme de la rédemption* (Louvain, 1931), 146-164; A. D'Ales, *La théologie de Tertullien* (Paris, 1905); R. Roberts, *The Theology of Tertullian* (London, 1924).

[24] On Cyprian, see J. Quasten, *Patrology* 2 (Utrecht, 1953), 340-383; A. Ehrhardt, *Polit. Metaphysik* 2. 159-181.

succeeded in holding the church of Carthage together as the sinking roman empire tried to pull it down in the maelstrom through which it was passing. But in saving Carthage, Cyprian secured the church in Africa, and strengthened that in Rome against destruction. [25]

He insisted that "outside the church there was no salvation," an axiom intended to demonstrate that in no philosophy such as that of Socrates or Plato, nor in the oriental cults represented by Hermes Trismigestus (*Ad idola* 6.23) was salvation to be had. He drew a further conclusion from the axiom, however, that immediately caused trouble. The sacraments, and particularly baptism performed by heretics, were invalid —a *nonsequitur* that Rome almost immediately repudiated; but with which the church down to Vatican Council II has had to contend. In its valid significance, the axiom is faultless. Outside of Christ's redemption that is embodied in the church, salvation is simply impossible. But to limit the extension of the church to its obviously visible members is to destroy the very idea of redemption that was performed once, and for all mankind, by Christ the Savior.

The problem came to a head when the confessors, who had suffered in the persecutions, and the martyrs-in-making claimed the powers of the priesthood to forgive sins. Cyprian had reacted with energy to insist that the bishop's and the priest's office had to be legitimately received through ordination before one could exercise such spiritual powers. He thus substantiated the traditional teaching of the church in regard to the spiritual power of the bishops as coming from Christ through the apostles in the church. But he himself ran into difficulty when he found that the african church, together with some churches in Asia Minor represented by Firmilian of Caesarea, could not agree with Rome and apparently the majority of bishops regarding the validity of heretically received baptism. Without going back on the source of episcopal power and legitimacy, and while he insisted on the idea of episcopal collegiality, he had to conclude that, in the final analysis, the bishop was

---

[25] Cf. H. Koch, *Cyprianische Untersuchungen* (Bonn, 1926), 1-78.

responsible directly to God. But within a visible organization such as the church that functioned as the body of Christ, this was not a fully sustainable thesis. [26]

On the other hand, Cyprian makes clear the type of organization that had developed in the exercise of episcopal powers, and gives ecclesiastical usage to the terminology common in juridical circles. He speaks of the *honor* due to the bishop; of the community acting *cum auctoritate et concilio*, "with the authority and advice" of the bishop; *sententiam dicere*—to render sentence; and finally he uses the word *decretum* or decree for the bishop's decision. All these terms quickly caught on and rendered the official status of the bishop clear and unmistakable. The result was a further clash with the roman state, whose rulers were convinced that they could not tolerate two bodies wielding authority over citizens, despite the fact that ecclesiastical authority claimed sanctions only in another world. [27]

The nature of the roman empire was such that any challenge to its total authority was looked upon as treason. This was a principal cause of the final persecutions under Diocletian and Licinius. Cyprian had foreshadowed his final conclusion when he wrote "[the apostate] has served his secular lord, observed his edict, and thereby obeyed a human command rather than God" (*De lapsis* 27). He saw the church as the "collected people of God," making no distinction between simple and gnostic christians, as did Clement of Alexandria and Origen. What is more, he traced the episcopal succession to Peter's successor rather than in the roman church as a whole. While he made a clear distinction between laity and the hierarchy, he did not misplace the rights of the former, frequently submitting important decisions to the judgment of a synod of clergy and laity, as two letters written from his hiding place in exile clearly demonstrate. This consultation of the laity had its climax in the election of the bishop, when the

---

[26] Cf. G. Bardy, *La théologie de l'église* 2 (Paris, 1947), 171-251; A. Ehrhardt, *op. cit.*, 163-165.

[27] A. Beck, *Römische Recht bei Tertullian* (Königsberg, 1930), 156ff.

Holy Spirit showed his choice through the suffrage of the laity and the testimony of the clergy (*Epist.* 44.3,2; 45,8,4). The principle would be enunciated in true roman fashion two hundred years later by Pope Leo I: "He who is to govern all, should be elected by all."

Cyprian's relationship with the state was governed primarily by his experience with the martyrs; and here his whole endeavor had been to strengthen the *militia Christi* in its resolve to resist force and corruption. In the true christian, he saw the presence of Christ that he compared to the juridical presence of the emperor in those exercising imperial power.

"If among the pagans it is a grand and glorious thing to have the proconsuls and emperor present among them, how much greater a factor, and loftier the glory it is to know that God and Christ is in our midst (*De opere* 21). If someone is preparing to enter a contest, he tries all the harder in view of the people and the emperor who will be present... but how much more glory and greater happiness do we experience when we take our places with God as the one presiding, and Christ as the one to crown us" (*Epist.* 58,8,1).

Cyprian's apparent neglect of the political factors in the roman rule other than his opposition to the tyranny of the persecution seemed to stem from his conviction that the end of the empire was at hand. It had begun as a kingdom with the murder of Remus by Romulus; it ceased as a republic with the murder of Caesar by Brutus; its disappearance was in order (*Ad idola* 5; *De lapsis* 2; *Epist.* 55,8,1). His opinion was based on the presumption that the *pax romana* was being gradually replaced by the *pax ecclesiae* and the peace of Christ with Almighty God as the "master of peace and concord" whose prototype was Christ.

In the end, Cyprian could see no use for a temple in a religion that considered the whole earth as the temple of God (*Ad idola* 9). The problem of Christ's silence before Pilate was resolved in the fact that Christ would speak on the last day in the judgment to be leveled on all of mankind; while the history of the passion in the church's expansion should encourage the martyrs in the spread of the kingdom of God (*Ad idola* 8).

114 *Politics and the Early Christian*

In the last resort, Cyprian conceived of christian politics as aimed at the kingdom of heaven in the next world.

> If it is praiseworthy for a soldier to return home in triumph after a victory, how much higher and greater is the praise of those who return to paradise after conquering the devil; and there, where Adam was caught as a sinner, to implant the victorious trophies of the ancient downfallen traitor?
> (*Ad fortunatum* 13).

6

The Constantinian Experiment

In the midst of the debacle suffered by the empire as a result of its interior crisis, the inroads of the barbarian peoples on the Rhone and Danube, and the persian pressure from the east, the emperor Diocletian assumed the supreme power in 284, and set about bringing order and territorial integrity to his vast realm.

A man of insight and genius, with a typical soldier's respect for the stabilizing quality of the older roman religion, he elevated Maximian as his co-regent in 285, and named two caesars in 286 to regularize governance and provide an orderly and peaceful precedent for the succession.

He likewise accepted the religious significance of the emperorship, proclaiming himself and his colleagues to be adoptively *diis geniti*, born to the gods. In his public monuments and coinage he was represented as Jovius (son of Jupiter) with Maximian as Herculius (son of Hercules), thus reverting to the tradition reinstated by Decius who had returned to the ancient roman deities, after divagations with the oriental gods, and particularly the mithraic worship of the second and early third century emperors. No great problem in credulity was involved here, as in both the roman state religion since the caesars, and in the mystery religions along with christianity that now prevailed all over the empire, god was a personal being whom the emperor represented, whether he was one or many. From

the pagan side at least, syncretistic borrowings were so frequent
as to be almost unremarked. [1]

In his attempt to preserve the integrity of the empire,
Diocletian found it necessary to assume the role of a total
dictatorship: in fiscal matters particularly, in the government
of the provinces, in securing the loyalty of the military, and
finally in the religious sphere, his laws became more severe
and absolute. Inevitably the final clash with christianity was
in the making, for whereas Celsus in *ca.* 180 had mocked the
lowly occupations of the faithful, by 270 Porphyry in his attack
on the church was concerned with the fact that it was a
stronghold of the rich, many of whom, by giving their goods
to the poor upon conversion, were upsetting the financial order
and destroying sources of fiscal revenue. [2]

By the turn of the fourth century, likewise, christians
occupied important governmental posts as magistrates, pro-
vincial governors, military commanders, and members of the
imperial household. But in carrying out their functions, they
were constantly forced into compromise. Since the state
religion was pagan, based upon loyalty to the gods, each official
function was accompanied by a religious ceremony, from the
oath-taking of the soldiers to the sacrifices at public spectacles
in which leading citizens were expected to participate. The
church considered all such activity as idolatrous. Hence the
Council of Elvira (*ca.* 304) in Spain listed a bill of particulars
condemning christian participation in these public functions. [3]

In March 297, Diocletian had published an edict condemning the manicheans as suspect of public crimes, since its
adherents rejected the practices of the state religion. But no
measures were taken against the christians as such, despite
minor incidents in the military, where a system of obligatory
conscription involved the christian in the oath-taking, or
violated his principles of non-violence. By 302 the problem

---

[1] Cf. E. Stein, *Histoire du Bas Empire* 1 (Paris, 1959); N. Baynes, *Cambridge Anc. Hist.*, 12 (1939), 646-667.
[2] Cf. Lactantius, *De morte persecutorum* 23; C. Cochrane, *Christianity and Classical Culture* (Oxford, 1944), 174-176.
[3] C. Bareille, *Dict. Théol. Cath.* 4 (1911), 2378-2397.

had grown large enough, however, to cause the emperor to expel christians from the army altogether. The next move was sudden and total.

Four edicts were published between February 303 and January 304 that forbade the exercise of the christian religion, confiscated the sacred books, and ordered the destruction of the christian churches. Finally, Diocletian decided on the imprisonment of the leaders of the church and, on a refusal to sacrifice to the gods, deportation or death. It was the logical development of a totalitarian political attempt to reconstitute the stabilization of the empire's integrity, as Diocletian and his colleagues conceived their task. It failed as such, but proved to be the immediate prelude to a revolutionary changeover in the religious adherence and complexion of the roman state. [4]

The persecutory edicts were applied with various force: lightly by Constantius Chlorus in the west; with great cruelty in the east. But by April 311, the emperor Galerius reluctantly recognized the futility of the policy and promulgated an edict of toleration at Nicomedia in Asia Minor. Despite an intensive application after the death of Galerius, Maximinus Daia also concluded that the fanatic loyalty of the christians to their faith was unbreakable. He too decided to establish religious peace in 312, a condition that was suggested for the west by Constantine and Licinius a short while earlier. In Italy and North Africa, Maxentius had ordered the restoration to the christians of the property confiscated during the persecutions, and this policy was also agreed upon by Licinius and Constantine in the beginning of 312, when they met in Milan for the marriage of Constantine's sister with Licinius.

Constantine set about the implementation of the agreement upon eliminating Maxentius after the famous victory near the Milvian bridge outside Rome on June 15, 313; and Licinius, though remaining a pagan, seems to have set about cultivating the favor of the christians in the east to offset the effects of the constantinian conversion that had followed the victory over

[4] J. Vogt, *Zur Religiosität der Christenverfolger* (Heidelberg, 1962); N. Baynes, *op. cit.*; W. Seston, *Mélanges Goguel* (Paris, 1950), 239-246.

Maxentius. Later, in the 320s, Licinius again returned to a policy of persecution probably to combat the christian adherence to Constantine's policies. But he was finally eliminated in 324, and Constantine became the sole emperor.

There is an insoluble problem involved in the motivation behind the constantinian religious changeover, and the quality of his christian conviction. In the story first recorded by Lactantius (*ca.* 318), and later repeated by Constantine's panegyrist Eusebius of Caesarea under the rubric of a confidence he had received directly from the emperor himself, Constantine's conversion was the result of a vision that he had on the eve of the battle. In this apparition, Christ assured him of victory, and advised him to mark his soldiers' shields with the christian chi-rho emblem ☧ or ☧. Whatever the resolution of the details, the fact is that the victory marked a definite turn-about in Constantine's political attitudes vis-à-vis the christian religion and its adherents. Despite the fact that he delayed his baptism until the eve of his death, and on occasion perpetrated highly unchristian deeds such as the assassination of his wife Fausta and son Crispus in 327, he did set about the christianization of the imperial rule and of a considerable part of the empire before his death in 337. [5]

Unchallengeable proof of this new policy is afforded by the christian symbols that appeared on the constantinian coinage beginning in 315, together with the disappearance of the pagan configurations after 323. [6]

Two basic laws were likewise inaugurated: one gave the church status as a privileged juridical corporation; the second recognized its property rights with the bishops empowered to exercise juridical functions even in matters involving purely civil jurisdiction. Thus the peace of the church was established, leading to a profusion of converts and the building of great churches in basilica form. The emperor's conversion also

---

[5] Cf. J. Vogt, "Bemerkungen zum Gang der Constantinforschung," *Mullus, Jahrb Ant. Christentum* 1 (1964), 374-379; F. X. Murphy, "Constantine I," *New Cath. Encyc.* (New York, 1967).

[6] Cf. M. Alföldi, "Die Sol-Comes-Münze von 325," *Mullus, op. cit.*, 10-16. *Die Constant. Goldprägung* (Mainz, 1963).

occasioned the development of theological disputes mainly as a result of the controversies that accompanied this sudden release and expansion of spiritual energy.

Two political theorists registered the development of this tremendous change: Lactantius, the latin rhetorician, who seems to have had a close connection with the emperor's thought at the beginning of his reign, and Eusebius of Caesarea, the great church historian and panegyrist who as an eastern bishop was privy to most of the emperor's activities at the height of his career, and laid the foundations for the interpretation of an imperially dominated, christian political order.

Lactantius (240-330) seems to have been converted to christianity about 300. Despite that fact, he had been employed by Diocletian as an instructor in the imperial household at Nicomedia where he seems to have had contact with the young Constantine. He was excluded from the palace when the persecution broke out, and returned to the west, where he wrote his *Divinæ institutiones* between 304 and 311. Dedicated to the emperor Constantine, the thesis of this tract is a justification of the presence of divine providence in the world. As a learned rhetorician, the author draws his material and proof from the writings of Cicero and the stoics, the sacred scriptures, the sybilline oracles, and the cosmic-oriented, religious literature attributed to Hermes Tresmigistus, as well as from Virgil and Ovid. His justification for this work results from his conclusion that the secular philosophy had failed since it proved to be an empty form without a true knowledge of divine truth, and in the end covered up rather than destroyed the evils in the world. [7]

In the political and social order, Lactantius maintained that he had followed the philosophers seeking justice, only to find that for the most part they had betrayed the natural order rather than discovered its true significance. He pointed to the communism praised by Plato as an example of this political

---

[7] Lactantius, *De morte per.* (ed. J. Moreau, Paris, Sour. chrét. 39, 1954); C. Cochrane, *Christianity and Cl. Culture*, 192-197.

ineptitude, maintaining that a true communism called not "for a community of fragile possessions, but for a community of minds" (*Div. inst.* 3.22). This common agreement on political and social ideals he discussed under the older philosophical concept of *humanitas* or true humanism. He saw in the stoic, eclectic philosophies a fear of human affection and the passions that caused the stoics in particular to cultivate the virtue of *apatheia*—the suppression of sensible emotions to favor contemplation of the one, the good, and the true. In this he saw an error that arose from the fact that these philosophers concentrated their efforts on the accomplishments of human reason without the aid of faith.

Despite the prevalence of war and hatred in human affairs —and he contrasted human relations with those of the animals, who, though by nature wild and ferocious, at least supposedly lived in peace within their own species—Lactantius saw the possibility of constructing a just republic based on the law of charity. He thus rejected the opinion of the political philosophers who traced the origin of states to a necessity for civic cooperation in obtaining food and mutual protection, or in civil contracts. He felt rather, as Augustine would later, that states were *latrocinia* or robber kingdoms. His solution was to introduce into the state an essentially stoic idea that he considered a christian principle. For Lactantius, the state was a gathering together of men for the sake of humanity *(humanitatis causa)*.

The foundation of true humanity was justice, the virtue that had as its primary postulate *philantropia* or love, one for another. Its constituent elements were *equitas* and *pietas;* but piety was not the Rome-vaunted virtue whereby a man reverenced his father *(pius est qui patrem dilexit*—he is pious who loves his father). It was rather love and devotion directed to the one true God, as the Father of all. The function of piety in the world was to provide a basis for the relations among men through love that came from God and led back to God. This is the principle behind the golden rule that is precisely a preparation for christian charity: "The basis of equity consists in not doing to another what you do not want done to you;

but measuring the feelings *(animum)* of another by your own" (5,15).

Without God, however, neither piety nor equity are possible. In the state, honors, rank, and power, despite Plato's opinion, are the rewards of injustice, for they have no relation to the justice of God. Lactantius further condemned the iniquity he found among men in society and the state, for he saw them as the result of rapine and conquest. Likewise wars were the result of envy, and the desire for imperialistic aggrandizement. They led inevitably to the destruction of humanity since they brought about the downfall and disruption of human nature.

By way of contrast, Lactantius lavished praise on the family as the root and source of life in society. But it is not the family in the roman juridical concept, with its legal constitution based on economic and property considerations. Rather it is the natural family formed through consanguinity and motivated by a devotion to the pursuit of virtue rather than the acquisition of property.

In the family each member is called upon not to eradicate his feelings and passions, but to subordinate them to the true purpose behind life: "the nature of man fleeing solitude and seeking after society and communication with his fellow-men..."[8]

The meaning behind the created world is summed up in the development of man and woman through the practice of virtue toward humanity; hence the law of God and that of the world demand that man discover within himself a heavenly and divine animal or being. In the new christian *polis* or state, opportunity should be given to the growth of the christian religion so that all men may be led to live a christian way of life. This requires freedom of religion for all men. Religion cannot be forced on anyone, but all should be coaxed into practising the truly christian virtues: hospitality, the redemption of captives, defense of widows, the care of the sick, and the burial of strangers.

---

[8] *De div. instit.* 5.5-7; cf. Cochrane, *op. cit.*, 194-195.

The sole justification for positive laws and the exercise of power on the part of the state is the existence of vice and ignorance among men. Here is where the roman genius could and should exercise humanity, thus bringing about a gradual evolution in the state whereby the law of love will replace that of vindictiveness. In all this Lactantius appears to have ignored a principal christian discovery, namely, the effects of an original blight on human nature—the fact that all men had sinned in Adam and required redemption in Christ. He is for all practical purposes a pelagian before the fact, neglecting the doctrine of grace. Apparently he saw in the christian religious ceremonies more the honor of God in the sense of the roman placating the gods by worship and imitation, than the permeation of the soul of the christian with a dynamic drive toward goodness, and a sharing in divine goodness itself that is constituted by grace.

On this score, Constantine's concept of christianity also was deficient; and though the emperor did magnificent things to embellish the external appearance of the new religion— building basilicas in Rome, Jerusalem, Trier, Nicomedia, and a whole new city at Constantinople; and while he preached the christian faith himself to his courtiers, [9] and legislated in favor of the christian moral law, he never seemed quite to have caught the inner significance of the mystery of salvation. Or maybe this is the true meaning of his reception of baptism on his death bed—that he felt until then unworthy of full reception into the mystery of salvation that was not shared by the majority of his subjects. This is possibly the result of the thinking of Lactantius, who maintained that the welfare of the state would come through man's free use of his true affections, through a shift in the principles behind the republic from the practical reason extolled by Aristotle, to the law and mercy preached by Christ.

Lactantius saw in the christian life of virtue the only sure means of achieving a better life, and did not seem to recognize

---

[9] On the significance of the constantinian construction program, see. J. Vogt, "Bemerkungen," *Mullus, op. cit.*, (1964), 378-379.

with St. Paul that conversion and baptism in Christ meant a
thorough revolution, a changeover from the *sarkic* or earth-
bound man to the spiritual, or Christ-oriented "new creature."
He was in the end merely a converted philosopher who believed
that the salvation of the roman people *(salus populorum roma-
norum)* could be brought about by a gradual amelioration of
the moral life of its subjects, combined with the bettering of
their social and living conditions. As such he seems to have
been the prophet to whom Constantine turned as he sought
a way to build a roman kingdom of God on earth with the
emperor as God's vice-regent, or as Eusebius would suggest,
as the new Moses or David.

Eusebius (260-340) was the father of church history, a truly
great literary practitioner and the theoretician behind a
theology of politics that had its inception at least in part with
Constantine, and was pursued in the byzantine empire from
the days of Zeno and Justinian to the fall of Constantinople.
It is Eusebius who saw in the conversion of Constantine the
opportunity for founding a christian *politeia* based upon what
he considered the obvious interventions of divine providence
in worldly affairs equivalent to God's speaking to the prophets
of old. He considered the emperor as the new Moses selected
by God to be the final lawgiver for the empire. He called the
emperor both an *isapostolus* or the equivalent of an apostle, and
a bishop *ton ekton*, "for those outside." But whether this latter
expression meant "those outside the church though living
within the empire," or the christians living under foreign
dominion, is not clear. To the former Constantine frequently
addressed himself encouraging their conversion. He acted as
protector for the latter in dealing particularly with the persian
monarch Sapor II. [10] But in both these missions he was not
successful. [11]

From the moment of his conversion likewise, he was con-

---

[10] Cf. F. Winkelmann, "Zur Geschichte des Authentizitätsproblem
der Vita Constantini," *Klio* (1962), 187-243; C. Cochrane, *op. cit.*, 183-212;
J. Vogt, "Constantinus I," *Real Ant. Christ.* 3 (195), 334.

[11] Cf. A. Jones, *Constantine and the Conversion of Europe* (New York,
Collier, 1962), 169-181.

fronted with a religious paradox. While he had hoped to
utilize the christian religion as a great instrument in achieving
the *pax romana* that was so urgently a function of his office as
emperor, he quickly discovered that the church itself was a
house divided. In 313 the donatist bishops in Africa wrote to
him demanding his intervention in their quarrel with the
catholics, for the restoration of their churches and properties.
The local governor had not recognized their claims upon
receiving imperial orders for the emancipation of the christians.
Constantine turned the problem over to a group of bishops
whom he instructed the bishop of Rome, Miltiades, to assemble
in the lateran palace that had been placed at the papal
disposition. On a second appeal from that decision, the
emperor suggested interpellating the gallic bishops at Arles in
314. He tried repression in 317; but in the end allowed the
quarrel to find its own solution. [12]

In similar fashion, the emperor expressed surprise and
indignation when he discovered the doctrinal dispute that had
broken out in Alexandria with Arius and the denial of the full
divinity of Christ. To settle this problem Constantine had the
bishops assemble at Nicea in 325, and while he took no direct
part in the debate, primarily, it would seem, because he could
not understand what he at first considered the nugatory
speculations of the heretic Arius, he did bring pressure to bear
on the final solution. It was with his assistance that the non-
scriptural term *homoousios* was used to connote the consubstantial natures of the Father and the Son that had been
apparently the contribution of Athanasius to the final settlement. Later Athanasius annoyed the emperor no little with
his intransigence in dealing with the arianizing bishops of the
east; and he was banished for his troubles.

But these theological difficulties were of no interest to the
emperor. He had wars to fight, cities to create, and the peace
of the empire to insure through the passing of practical laws
for the exclusion of rabble-rousing heretics and jews, and the

---

[12] Cf. W. Frend, " Constantine's Settlement with the Church, " *Modern
Churchman* 6 (London, 1962), 32-64.

punishment of malefactors. In the end, for all the efforts of his panegyrist, Eusebius, Constantine proved more of a Solomon than a David; and God seemed to have dealt with his sons in a fashion modeled on the fate of the sons of Solomon. In an *Oration* attributed to him by Eusebius he had spoken of the *instinctu divinitatis, mentis magnitudo*—prodding of divinity and greatness of mind—with which he felt called to the tremendous task of renovating his world through the christian religion.

His wish was to demonstrate the divine assistance through victories in war and the obvious justice of the christian *politeia:* "So that it would come about through divine favor in our regard, such as we have experienced in so many instances, that He will preserve [the roman state] in prosperity for our successors to the end of time." [13]

Julian the Apostate (360-363) saw the incongruity of his illustrious though despised uncle's desires when he accused Constantine of carrying about the christian *labarum* or war emblem in the final struggle with Licinius, as the jews had carried the ark of the tabernacle into battle.

The total incongruity of the constantinian position was experienced by his son Constantius II (335-361) who in 352, after a series of fratricidal experiences, found himself sole emperor. Desirous of following his father's footsteps in making christianity the sole religion of the realm, he attempted to support its claims by legislating severely against the pagan superstitions, their sacrifices and magical practices, particularly divinizations and astrology. He liberated the christian priests and their families and servants from the extraordinary taxes and services demanded by the state of its ordinary citizens. These included the requirement of harboring soldiers, and working on public projects and roads. He granted special immunities to all those who gave service in the hospitals and houses for the poor that had appeared in many of the cities as a consequence of a newly cultivated christian addiction to the corporal works of mercy. [14]

---

[13] C. Cochrane, *op. cit.*, 183 and n. 1.
[14] Cf. J. Moreau, "Constantius II," *Real Antike u. Christ.* 2 (1959), 162-179.

At the same time, however, primarily due to the tremendous financial deficit suffered by the empire as a result of its wars against the barbarians, and the repudiation of their financial burdens by many senators and wealthy landowners, he was forced to pass stringent laws binding the decurions and municipal officials to their positions in the cities.

Gradually, likewise, it became necessary to impose fixed services to the state on the local officials and their sons: the people engaged in supplying food and grain from the public lands, the transportation and distribution officials, as well as the cultivators of the land, and the corporations of sailors, producers, and merchants; even the sculptors and painters were bound to their professions. These laws and regulations were the desperate effort of a man charged with holding the line within a dying civilization.

Unfortunately, the sudden introduction of christianity as a new force that might have helped to save the situation had served rather to complicate it the more. For the constantinian concept had not been revolutionary enough. And among the christian leaders there was both confusion and, what was worse, heresy.

While Constantine had considered the arguments of Arius as merely logical difficulties, in actual fact they were substantial objections against the trinitarian concept. And it was only on the acceptance of a triune God that the christian could proclaim the divinity of Christ, and what followed from that doctrine concerning the eradication of the old man through baptism in Christ's death, and his "new creation" in the resurrection which was the true and inner meaning of the initiation into christianity. The emperor and his successor missed this significance. Constantius II certainly favored the arian cause, whether on purely political principles or because he liked the logic of its position.

But in actual fact, while logical, the arian position was simply a betrayal of the true christian message; and the men who opposed it incontinently, such as Athanasius of Alexandria, Hilary of Poitiers, and Basil of Cappadocia understood fully the total necessity of the battle in which they were engaged.

This is not to assert that, had the christian faith been accepted in its full significance, it would have saved the empire. Tertullian had disposed of that hope a full century earlier when he remarked: "It was impossible to immix the imperial rule with the reign of Christ, even should the emperor believe in Christ, or christians become caesars" (*Apol.* 21). The observation was concurred in by another great churchman whose experience with the constantinian experiment gave him the right to formulate valid observations. After the council of Milan in 355, writing to Constantius the aged bishop Ossius of Cordova had summoned the courage to warn the emperor :

> "Do not use force, "he said, "send us no letters or counts....
> Under Constans, what bishops suffered banishment? When did
> he appear as arbiter in an ecclesiastical trial? When did any pa-
> latine official of his compel men to subscribe against anyone? ....
> Cease these proceedings, I beg you, and remember that you are
> a mortal man. Take unto your accounting the day of judgment
> and keep yourself uncontaminated in anticipation of that event.
> Do not intrude yourself into ecclesiastical affairs; nor give us orders
> about them. But instead learn from us. God has placed the
> empire in your hands; but to us he has entrusted the affairs of
> his church. Thus, as whoever would try to usurp your reign
> would be resisting the ordinance of God, so you should likewise
> concern yourself against committing a great offense by interfering
> in the government of the church". [15]

[15] Athanasius, *Apol.* 6; *Contra arianos* 46; cf. J. De Clercq, *Ossius of Cordoba* (Washington, 1954), 445-458.

7

Athanasius to Chrysostom

In Athanasius of Alexandria (337-361) Constantius II, like his father before him, found an implacable anti-arian whose theological competence and ascetical propaganda had a tremendous effect upon the church, particularly in the west, where he spent long years as part of the five exiles to which he was subjected. He repudiated a philosophical treatment of the trinity and the incarnation, insisting that these mysteries could only be understood in the context of a biblical theology. He pointed out that a philosophical approach to the supreme being as the cause of causes—or the *arche*—could only lead to some type of pantheism *(Cont. gentes)*.

His doctrinal reliance was centered on St. Paul, who had discovered a true knowledge of God and of sacred things in the reflection of Christ's sayings and doings in this world that he recognized as a recapitulation of divine revelation through the scriptures.

Athanasius combined political astuteness with theological competence and a fearlessness that merited both the admiration of his contemporary, the pagan historian, Ammianus Marcellinus, and of the eighteenth century literary agnostic, Edmund Gibbon, who referred to his career as "Athanasius against the world." His absolute refusal to accept deposition from the see of Alexandria, and his utilization of the monks to secure his hold on his diocese, enabled him to gain gradual civil control of the whole of Egypt, preparing the way for the pharaoh-like rule of his successors such as Theophilus and Cyril of Alexandria. This was not his direct purpose, but it is an indication of his political competence. He was the first churchman to prepare a letter of political propaganda signed by fellow bishops and circulated in contravention of the emperor's policies; and his direct attacks on the arians in his *De synodis* and *Contra arianos* were documented with full, though partly questionable, historical facts and citations, that gave them a probative weight which no amount of argumentation on the part of his enemies could overcome.

In his *Life of St. Anthony* Athanasius combined the credulous and philosophical temper of the day with an overload of folkloristic demonology that reached deep into the psychological beliefs of his contemporaries, particularly in the west; and that gave impetus to a great and lasting ascetical movement —Augustine was one of its products—no matter what may have been the weird reactions of an Anatole France and other decadent, late 19th century litterateurs. His political insight led him to believe that there could be no true union between the divinely revealed history of salvation that should promote man to deification in preparation for the resurrection, and the pursuit of the political necessities and ideals even of the secular state. There was no possibility of combining the kingdom of Christ with the roman empire. [1]

Athanasius approached the legal status of the christian in the empire on theological and soteriological principles in the footsteps of Origen. He maintained that with the redemption, the true believer was incorporated through baptism into the sacramental life of Christ's body, the church. He therefore came under the immediate tutelage of the bishops, who were "the stewards of the divine mysteries."

Hence it was only in purely secular affairs that the christian was subject to the emperor. For the emperor to interfere with matters of faith was a sacrilegious act and intolerable. His

---

[1] Cf. J. Quasten, *Patrology* 3 (Utrecht, 1960), 20-79; E. Schwartz, *Zur Geschichte des Athanasius* (Berlin, de Gruyter, 1959); K. Setton, *Christian Attitude toward the Emperor* (New York, 1941), 67-83; 198-199; C. Cochrane, *Christianity and Cl. Culture*, 257-260; 361ff.

competence was described by St. Paul, and confined by Christ to matters having to do with the public order and the well-being of the state. Where a conflict between ecclesiastical and secular affairs arose, the bishops should be consulted before the civil or criminal side of the action was implemented. But the emperor should refrain from theological decisions, or favoring heretical causes in the formation even of a christian empire. [2]

Despite a preliminary hopefulness akin to that of Eusebius, the bishop of Alexandria's own experiences with the state quickly convinced him that the constantinian experiment, at least as conceived by Eusebius of Caesarea who saw in the emperor a new Moses or David, and who had desired to create a christian theocracy, was not to be an authentic expression of the city of God.

For Athanasius the church, and not the state, was a body in which the "doctrine of the mysteries" was confirmed; and in which the true faith was lived by the saints from one generation to another; the church alone preserved the true impress and image of Christ in the world. Spread throughout the universe, the church taught the same faith, held to the same worship, and was sustained by the sacramental union between the Redeemer and the redeemed.

While the administrative order expressed in the canons of tradition gave a visible character to the church, it was still the faith and not law that gave the church its cohesiveness. Thus the element that united the bishops was a common office of preserving the faith. According to Athanasius, it was God who raised bishops to the episcopate *(Contr. arianos 6)* making them, like Christ, the "bishops or overseers of souls." Hence the bishop, though mortal, was given to the faithful for their spiritual welfare, and he was married to his church. On this score Athanasius had admonished the monk Dracontius, who was reluctant to accept the bishopric after his election by the people, that he had no right to be selfishly thinking of his own

---

[2] Athanasius, *Hist. arianorum* 52; 74-75; cf. C. Cochrane, *op. cit.*, 258-260.

salvation, since his achievement of the highest spiritual goals was now bound up with feeding and protecting the flocks of Christ *(Epist. ad Drac.)*.

In summing up the principles that inform the church, Athanasius maintained that Christ had come to witness the truth and thereby to destroy the work of the devil *(Contra arian.* 2.51); that he had gathered together all the nations, and by freeing all men from sin, had made all sons of God *(Ibid.,* 2.72). His purpose was fulfiled in his death and resurrection; but his liberation of man from death and sin was only possible because Christ was truly God and truly man. And both these truths had to be maintained. Christ's manhood was necessary so that all mankind would participate with and through him in the redemption; but the redemption itself was impossible if Christ was not consubstantial—*homoousios*—with the Father. With this crystal-clear theological notion, there could be no compromise. And when the civil ruler, and Constantius II in particular, attempted to interfere in the belief of the church, the bishops had no choice but to oppose him. [3]

In the mind of the emperor, of course, the primary objective of his government was to achieve peace throughout his realm. Influenced by the bishops in his immediate entourage, Constantius II attempted to secure universal approval for the arian creed by force. However, it was precisely here that he ran into the vigorous and inviolable resistance of Athanasius and his supporters. At the synod of Milan in 355, Constantius tried to force the metropolitan bishops of Trier (Paulinus), Cagliari (Lucifer), and Milan (Denis) to subscribe to the condemnation of Athanasius and enter into communion with the arians. On their refusal, he responded that they should accept "his imperial decision as a canon of the church." The bishops instead, though threatened with exile, "warned him against infringing on ecclesiastical order, and mingling roman imperial sovereignty with the constitution of the church" (Athan., *Hist. arian.* 33 and 34).

---

[3] Cf. K. Morrison, "Rome and the City of God," *Transactions Amer. Phil. Society* 54.1 (Phila., 1954), 28-30; 35-40.

This same caution was expressed even more clearly in the letter of pope Julius to the arians after the synod of Rome. For Julius, the church was an institutional body discrete from the state, an *isopoliteia*, whose constitution was founded on the faith and the sacraments. The emperor's only function in church affairs was to enable the proper ecclesiastical courts to discharge their duties. [4]

HILARY OF POITIERS

The experience of Hilary of Poitiers and the principles of ecclesiastical independence that he enunciated were almost identical with those of Athanasius. He attributed the freedom of the christian, as man and citizen, to his release from the captivity of sin by being established in the body of Christ's flock through baptism and the sacraments. "For he is the church, holding it all within himself, through the sacrament of his body" (*Tract. in Ps.* 125.6). It is then above all by the confession of Christ as the Son of God, and by a sincere participation in his body through the sacraments, that the true character of the believer is established, and the source of ecclesiastical unity is certified. [5]

At the center of Hilary's faith is the confession of Peter: "You are the Christ, son of the living God" (*De Trinitate* 2,23). As God then, Christ had condescended to assume the form of a servant; and as a man, to sacrifice himself for the redemption of mankind. In that redemption was achieved true liberty.

Hilary admitted that the civil authority had a part to play in ecclesiastical affairs where it might be required for good order, or for the implementation of the decisions of the bishops. In fact he accepted the banishment imposed on him by the empire in execution of his condemnation by an earlier synod (*Ad Constant.* 2). But once the emperor overstepped his

---

[4] Cf. E. Schwartz, *op. cit.*, 292-301; K. Morrison, *op. cit.*, 11.
[5] K. Morrison, *op. cit.*, 28-39; S. Greenslade, *Church and State from Constantine to Theodosius* (London, 1954), 41-44; A. Feder, Coll. Antiariana *CSEL* 65 (1916), 181-187; W. Parsons, "Early Patristic Political Thought," *Theol Stud.* 1 (1940), 358-359.

competence and meddled in matters of faith, he lost his right
to obedience; and, with Hilary in the end, to respect.

In his first two letters to the emperor written from exile,
Hilary apparently presumed that Constantius was sincere in
his search for the truth; but that he was being misinformed by
the perversity of the bishops surrounding him. In his first
Address to the Emperor, that is actually only a résumé of the
synod of Sardica (348), Hilary complained vehemently that
the freedom of the church was intruded upon; for while the
emperor's duty was to ensure for his subjects the benefit of
liberty, in actual fact the civil judges acting for the emperor
had intruded themselves into ecclesiastical affairs; they had
tormented innocent men, depriving clerics of their rights. He
begged the emperor to correct these evils, and to allow the
people to follow their rightful ecclesiastical leaders in peace,
and to celebrate the divine mysteries in an orthodox fashion.
They in return would pray for the welfare of the emperor. [6]

Hilary continued this argument in his second address to
the emperor. He maintained that, with the banishment of
Athanasius and Eusebius of Vercelli, the arians had been able
to imperil the "hope, life, and immortality of all men." For
they retained the appearance of baptism, but deprived it of
all meaning, since they denied that Christ is truly God—"as if
baptism could be something without faith in Christ." He
requested an audience with the emperor, since the welfare of
mankind was at stake; and in the end he did not hesitate to
use the word *antichrist* for anyone—and this did not exclude
the emperor—who refused to confess Christ as the only-
begotten God (*Ad Constant.* 3-5, 7, 8, 11).

In a further, third address, written apparently after the
death of the emperor, Hilary condemned Constantius as the
antichrist himself. He had attempted to subvert the faith
while giving the impression of favoring piety. His persecution
was at once more subtle and more insidious than those of old.
By lavishing immunities and the remission of taxes on the
clergy, by allocating revenues to the churches, by honoring

---

[6] S. Greenslade, *op. cit.*, 42; K. Morrison, *op. cit.*, 30.

servile bishops and promoting flatterers, the emperor had all but destroyed the inner fabric of the faith. Good prelates he banished and abused. He had torn bishops from the altar in Milan; reviled those of Trier and Rome; and desecrated church and clergy in Toulouse. It was the emperor who manipulated the heretical revisions of the creed that deviated from the faith of Nicea; and he had starved out the synod of Rimini until its important bishops accepted the arian formula. It was Constantius who with threat and violence had splintered the synod of Seleucia, splitting the church in two, and making a present to his master, the devil, of the world for which Christ had died. Faithless, the emperor had promulgated the faith; impious, he had dissembled piety; with edicts, he had terrorized truth *(Contra Constant.)*.

In the long run, however, Hilary did not deny the jurisdiction of the emperor in regulating those things that belonged to God but touched on the province of caesar. What he called for was a clear distinction between the requirements of the public order, and what was of faith; and he saw as a consequence of the faith the emperor's function as guaranteeing the liberty of bishops and faithful to practice their religion in an uncontaminated fashion. [7]

JULIAN THE APOSTATE

From premises of a completely different theology, Julian the Apostate (361-63) agreed with Athanasius and Hilary. He had barely escaped assassination with his cousins after the death of Constantine in 337 A.D., and was brought up in so suffocating an atmosphere of repression that he formed a thorough hatred for everything christian. Once he got to Athens and the university—he was a contemporary there of the cappadocians, Gregory Nazianzen and Basil—he turned totally to the pagan philosophy. Become emperor in 361, he set about turning the clock back on christianity, announcing his program as a return to the policy of Constantinus Chlorus.

------

[7] K. Morrison, *ibid.*, 30-31.

He accused the christians of both superstition and hypocrisy, and expelled their teachers from the schools on the pretext that they could not possibly square their consciences with giving instruction in greek or latin letters, since the pagan literature was essentially dominated by the myths and stories of the gods. [8]

Assuming the role of a great emancipator, he liberated all the christian bishops in exile, in the hope that upon return to their dioceses they would provoke new internal strife. Proclaiming himself a philosopher-ruler, he instructed the people to follow the ancient, virtuous life of true citizens by cultivating liberty, independence, justice, temperance, and fortitude to achieve the prudence that became the intelligent hellenic citizen of a great empire.

He himself lived as a true neoplatonist, believing that the god of nature governed all things by fortune and fate; and he practiced the virtues of purity and chastity—after the death of his wife, he lived in continence. [9]

He proclaimed a *pax juliana*, and punished malefactors with pagan exactitude. He abolished the privileges of the christian priesthood, and attempted to reorganize the old pagan cults. While he did not authorize a persecution of the church, he insinuated his desire to downgrade christianity. Ammianus Marcellinus described him thus: "While occasionally he might react intemperately in an argument, he would inquire at another time concerning the opinions of his opponents; but never would he permit a departure from the truth even in dispute, and he could never be accused of deviating in religion or any other form of equity" (22.10.2). Julian's writings were numerous, and on the point of death, after being wounded in battle, he declared himself content to die, since he had never deflected in his pursuit of the will of god, nor of the well-being of the state or its citizens. The christian propagandists of the next age branded him an apostate, which he was; and they took little notice of the ideals he had striven to follow. But

---

[8] C. Cochrane, *op. cit.*, 261-291; K. Morrison, *op. cit.*, 27-28.
[9] C. Cochrane, *op. cit.*, 290-291.

his works had to be refuted half a century later by Cyril of Alexandria, so powerful a hold did they have on the pagan thinkers of the next generation. [10]

BASIL OF CAPPADOCIA

The death of Julian in 363 brought to the throne the soldier Jovian, selected by the army. He was an orthodox christian who evidently believed in religious toleration. He was succeeded by Valentinian I, of whom Ammianus Marcellinus remarked: "Because he stood in the middle of the different religions, he disturbed no one; and did not order the observance of any particular cult" (30.9). This testimony is supported by a law of 371 granting freedom of worship to all. Since Valentinian accepted the nicene faith, the emperor tried to favor the church by increasing the privileges of the clergy. But when the eastern bishops requested him to summon a council, he is said to have replied: "I am of the laity; and therefore I have no right to interfere in such affairs. Let the bishops who are concerned with these matters assemble where they please" (Sozomen, *Hist. eccl.* 6.7). And although the donatists in Africa complained that they were actually being persecuted by Romanus, Valentinian did not interfere until, in 373, he was forced to do so when they joined the rebellion of Firmus. [11]

His associate Valens tolerated paganism in the east but was arian in sympathy, owing apparently to the influence of the bishop of Constantinople, Eudocius. His great opposition came from the cappadocian fathers, particularly Basil and Gregory Nazianzen. Of a well-to-do family, educated in Athens and Constantinople, and traveled, Basil had functioned as a rhetor before his final conversion to an ecclesiastical way of life. He had attempted a modified type of monasticism on his family property; but finally found his ecclesiastical vocation was in the active sphere. He did, however, prepare a series of rules

---

[10] P. Rigazzoni, "Il contra Galilaeos dell' Imperatore Giuliano," *Didaskaleion* 6 (1928), 1-114.

[11] C. Cochrane, *op. cit.*, 293-317.

for regulating the lives of monks and nuns as part of the christian *eunomia*. He went further in his desire to prescind from the more rational type of morality that had led to ascetical extremism with Eustathius of Sebaste, one of Basil's earlier mentors, or that settled for a strictly legalistic approach to holiness.

In his *Moralia*, Basil reached back to the gospels for specific direction in making up one's conscience on what should be thought, said, and done. Then, as bishop of Caesarea in Cappadoccia, he set about organizing institutions for the true christianization of the *polis*. Basil felt that the faithful should serve as a leaven for the whole of society. Thus he established monasteries close to a parish or diocese, each with a superior holding absolute authority, chosen by the monks of surrounding monasteries. Scripture study for the learned and manual labor for the uncultivated were the occupation of the monks; these activities were to be blended into their liturgical functions and care of the poor. He next established orphanages and schools in connection with the monasteries, and eventually houses for the infirm and the aged. But all these enterprises were under the control of the bishop with a central administration. Eventually, they formed a small city in themselves, and were referred to as Basiliads. [12]

During the famine of 367 A.D., Basil, while still a priest, had been called upon by his bishop to both preach against the avarice of the rich, and to organize relief stations for the destitute. This experience fashioned his thought with regard to property rights and social justice; and in sermons on *The Rich*, on *Avarice*, on *In Time of Famine and Need*, and against *Usury*, he drove home the fact that every man had an inalienable right to a living—a right that was not to be violated by the claims of property or possessions; and in the case of conflict, private rights must cede before common needs. As bishop, he pursued this policy in his relation with civil officials; and

---

[12] Cf. J. Quasten, *Patrology* 3, 204-236; F. X. Murphy, Patristic Portrait : "Basil the Cappadocian," *Catholic World* 157 (1943), 278-287; R. Deferrari- M. McGuire, *The Letters of St. Basil*, 4 vols. (Loeb Cl. Lib, reprint 1950).

in his letters there is a constant echo of requests to governors for the remission of taxes and other imposts in favor of the deprived and dispossessed, and the redress of injuries for the impoverished. [13]

Basil had inherited from Athanasius the task of withstanding the arianizing of the east; and in the emperor Valens he found himself up against a new Constantius II. But so powerful a figure had he become that he was described by Gregory of Nazianzen in his funeral oration as having confronted the governor Modestus, surprised at Basil's blunt refusal of an imperial order with the remark, "Evidently you have never yet met a catholic bishop!" While he did not discuss the relations between church and empire as such, Basil did everything in his power to circumvent the intrusion of the civil administration in church affairs. He arranged new dioceses and consecrated bishops, and appealed, vainly it seems, to pope Damasus in Rome for assistance. While in his writings before his great treatise on the Holy Spirit—whose theological thought was canonized at the Council of Constantinople in 381, two years after Basil's demise—he had practiced *condescension* or mercifulness, by not forcing the eunomian dissenters to the wall of heresy. But he had seen the absolute significance of the trinitarian doctrine in the christian faith, and its meaning in the political sphere. [14]

There had been no question in Basil's mind of challenging the emperor's right to rule; and all during this period, down to the beginning of the middle ages and beyond, the churchmen, including the popes, felt they were essentially citizens of the empire. This fact is made clear by Optatus of Milevis, the catholic bishop in Africa embroiled with the donatists. When the latter asked, "What has the emperor to do with the church?", Optatus tried to explain that the church was within the state, and not the state within the church. "No one," he

---

[13] D. Nothomb, "Charité et Unité, Doctrine de S. Basile," *Proche Orient chrétien* 4 (1954), 310-321; E. Brück, *Kirchenväter und Erbrecht* (Cologne, 1956), 3-10; S. Giet, *Les idées et l'action sociale de S. Basile* (Paris, 1941); B. Treucker, *Polit. u. sozialgeschichtliche Studien zu den Basilius Briefen* (Frankfort, 1961).

[14] Cf. G. Reilly, *Imperium and Sacerdotium in St. Basil* (Washington, 1945).

added, "is above the emperor except God alone who made him emperor." At the end of the fourth century, likewise, the unknown author of the Ambrosiaster wrote in his commentary on St. Paul: "The king is honored *(adoratur)* on earth as if he were the vicar *(quasi vicarius)* of God." He went further and maintained: "The king has the image of God, just as the bishop has that of Christ". [15]

While more retiring and self-centred than St. Basil, his companion of youth, Gregory Nazianzen led a life of modest pastoral care for the people of the diocese attached to his name, though he was actually consecrated for the town of Sasima. He had also served for a year (381-382) as bishop of Constantinople in the midst of great political and ecclesiastical turmoil. His reflections on political theory were strictly in an ecclesiological perspective, as he informed the local magistrates of Nazianzus, "You rule along with Christ, and with him you minister your office. From him you have received the sword, not to use it, but to threaten its use ... You are the image of God; but you also rule over the image of God, destined for another life" *(Orat.* 17.9). At the same time, he assured the people that the bishop exercised power under the law of Christ with an authority more important than that of earthly rulers since it touched on celestial things. [16]

Epiphanius of Salamis (315-403), the great fourth century traveler and hunter of heretics, quoting Paul's *Epistle to the Romans,* maintained that the right of vindictive action on the ruler's part came directly from God, but that his function was to establish "the proper and well-ordered rule of the whole world." He seemed to imply that in man's nature, besides the factor of sin, there was a requirement for society to be governed in accord with God's plan for mankind *(Ad. haer.* 40.4). These various theories and observations were to be tested as by fire in the experiences of a great churchman and

---

[15] Ambrosiaster, *Dissertiones* 91.35, *CSEL* 50. 63, 157; W. Parsons, *op. cit.,* 359-360; R. and A. Carlyle, *History of Mediaeval Political Theory* 1, 149.

[16] J. Quasten, *Patrology* 3, 236-254; F. Dvornik, *Late Classical and Mediaeval Studies in Honor of A. Frend* (Princeton, 1955), 71-80.

supreme orator, John Chrysostom, whose competence lay in the field of action, commenting directly on the gospel as he tried to cope with the necessities of the economic, social, and political life of the church in both Antioch and Constantinople at the start of the fifth century.

JOHN CHRYSOSTOM

The contribution of John Chrysostom to the development of the christian political thought was considerable, both in his own example of "obeying the higher authorities" and in his opposition to the injustice of the imperial court and the high-handed behavior of ecclesiastical courtiers and bishops. As a well-known preacher who had exercised both his priestly prudence and oratorial powers to prevent a general riot in Antioch, he was summoned to Constantinople and consecrated bishop at the behest of the imperial court. Acting with the *parrhesia*, or fearless courage, that St. Paul indicated as proper to the regenerated christian, Chrysostom execrated the evils of the court. He was twice exiled for his efforts, and died in destitution at Comana in the Comus mountains of northern Asia Minor in 404 A.D., after suffering ill-treatment at the hands of ecclesiastical officials in the person of Theophilus of Alexandria, and of the empress Eudoxia. His conduct and reputation were quickly exonerated at the insistence of Rome, and his bones were returned to Constantinople for honorable burial by Theodosius II. [17]

In several of his sermons, as well as in his great Commentary on the Epistles of St. Paul, Chrysostom had approached the problem of the imperial authority in relation to the christian conscience and the church. As a man of his age, he had accepted the fact that the ecclesiastical authority was within, and not above the empire; and in his Commentary on Romans, he laid down the principle that the highest authorities in the church were bound to obey the civil authorities (*Hom. rom.* 23).

---

[17] Cf. C. Baur, *John Chrysostom and His Times*, 2 vols. (London, 1959); J. Quasten, *Patrology* 3, 421-482.

In support of this conviction, he cited Paul's "Let every soul be subject to the higher powers," and maintained that this had reference to the priest, the prophet, and apostle, as well as to the ordinary citizen.

For Chrysostom the key to this theory was supplied by the pauline "be subject, since there was no power but from God." However he made it clear that the ruler had not been appointed directly by God, but that it was God's power that was utilized by the one possessing authority. And he pointed out the fact that obedience to the state was perfectly in keeping with man's dignity, since in being subject to earthly power, the christian was obeying God who established that power. In this sense, the citizen was paying a debt of justice to his maker.

Chrysostom discussed the duties of the ruler, who served as God's minister in presiding over peace in the state:

> To no small degree they contribute
> to the present tranquility by keeping
> guard, beating off enemies, restraining
> sedition in the cities, and by terminating
> differences among factions. It is not
> to the misuse of authority, but to the good
> order that is in the institution itself,
> that attention should be turned. [18]

Apparently following Aristotle, the bishop of Constantinople traced the establishment of secular authority to "an agreement among men that rulers should be maintained by us; their worth consists in the fact that, to the neglect of their personal affairs, they look after the public welfare, spending all their time in safeguarding the goods of others." [19]

In his homily on *Empire, Power, and Glory*, he developed this idea further, asserting that divine wisdom arranged the relationship of ruled to rulers, in order to prevent disorderliness, and that the peoples should not be tossed about like waves.

---

[18] *Hom. in Rom.* 23; cf. W. Parsons, *op. cit.*, 353-358.
[19] *Ibid.*, 355.

If you remove the helmsman, you sink the boat. Take the general from an army, and you betray the soldiers to the enemy; deprive the state of its rulers, and the people will live a life more irrational than that of the beasts ... Hence the good ruler uses his power to reward or punish his subjects. [20]

In his *Commentary on Genesis*, Chrysostom distinguished three kinds of human subjection: that used in relation to women; to slaves; and a much more formidable dominion, "the result of sin." This was the subjection St. Paul had in mind when he said: "If you do what is evil, fear; for not without cause does he [the ruler] carry the sword" (Rom 13,3-4). Because of man's depravity, therefore, government came into existence; and Paul confirmed this fact when he asserted that "the law is not made for the just man" (I Tm 1,9).

Chrysostom thus seemed to agree that it was because of sin that law was required for the well-being of society; and that if man were living in a state of innocence, there would be no need of human authority. On the other hand, he placed no great trust in the ruler merely because he possessed this authority. "The emperor is a man as we are," he informed his listeners. "He is endowed with the same feelings that we have; and he has the same soul." (*Hom. ad pop. Antioch.* 7.2).

In comparison with the courtly flattery poured on the person of the emperor by contemporary philosophers such as Libanios and Themistios, Chrysostom was mild in the terminology of respect that he applied to the rulers. In fact, his final loyalty was to a higher authority, that of the church as impersonating Christ, and that of the bishop, devoutly dealing with spiritual power.

"The bishop is also a ruler," he maintained, "and indeed more worthy of honor than the emperor. For the holy laws of the spiritual authority of the bishop render the person of the emperor subject to him" (*Hom. ad pop. Antioch 3.2*).

Since the priest judges things on earth that have their

---

[20] *Ibid.*, 356.

immediate repercussion in heaven, therefore "God has subjected even the person of the king to the power of the priest, in order to teach us that his power is greater."

There were those who did not appreciate Chrysostom as bishop, and in the end decided to prove to him that the emperor's power was the mightier, at least here on earth; consequently John Chrysostom died in exile. But his life and doctrine were vindicated at the demand of the roman see by Theodosius II, the son of his persecutors, Arcadius and Eudoxia, with the return of his ashes to Constantinople on January 27, 438. His teaching played a part in the subsequent thousand years of struggles between the emperors and the church that was involved in the history of the great byzantine state from Justinian I (518-565) to the fall of Constantinople in 1453. They still have a bearing on modern social and political thought. This fact was acknowledged by the great nineteenth century churchman John Henry Newman who confessed that he "loved Chrysostom as a brother!" They are in need today of a more profound elucidation than is possible here.

8

The Age of Theodosius

An indication of the complexity of the religious and cultural situation that followed the death of Julian the Apostate and the accession to the supreme rule of the empire of Jovian (363-64), then of Valentinian I and Valens, is furnished by the pagan historian Ammianus Marcellinus. He had manifested little enthusiasm for the reactionary program of Julian, but at the same time did not consider accepting the new christian order. Ammianus had the merit of attempting to depict both Julian and his successor Valentinian in their true colors; and he has nought but praise for the latter, under whose regime, he testifies, all persons received the protection due to their rank and station excepting alone those guilty of treason (Amm. 28.1).[1]

Ambrose, later in his quarrel with Symmachus, would likewise appeal to the laws of Valentinian to assert the christian toleration "was of long duration," granting religious liberty to all citizens (*Epist.* 1.17; *Relat. ad Sym.* 3). Ammianus considered Valentinian an excellent ruler betraying weakness only in

---

[1] On Ammianus as an historian, see M. Laistner, *The Later Roman Historians* (Berkeley, Calif., 1947), 141-164; on the political thought during this period, cf. C. Cochrane, *Christianity and Classical Culture* (New York, Oxford, 1944), 292-357; A. Alföldi, *A Conflict of Ideas in the Late Roman Empire* (Valentinian I), (Oxford, 1952); W. Ensslin, *Die Religionspolitik des Kaisers Theodosius der Grosse* (Sitzbr. Bayer. Akad. 1953, 2); S. Greenslade, *Church and State from Constantine to Theodosius* (London, SMC, 1954, 64-78).

dealing with tough military leaders; and he depicts Valens as stern and honest (27.9,4; 31.14,2-3).

Conscious that the revival of *romanitas* attempted by Julian had been just as disastrous as the attempted theocracy under Constantius II, Valentinian had sought to implement the principle of toleration by confirming the christian legal exemptions and immunities, while condemning the abuse of ecclesiastical privileges, and concurrently by legitimizing the traditional greek and roman cults. These included the hellenic mysteries, but excluded divinization except in its traditional latin cultic form. Both the astrological extravagances of the *mathematici* or diviners, and the deleterious religious practices of the manichees were proscribed.

While Valentinian attempted to dissociate the bishops from political activity, and to keep the politicians from acting as bishops, he did not abrogate the empire's right to interfere even in questions of doctrine when they obviously affected the public order. On the other hand, his main occupation was the defense of the west; while his colleague Valens attempted to protect the frontiers of the east, concentrating his attention on the Danube. So great was the strain put upon the empire by the reorganization of its military forces and the stabilizing of its finances that frequent attempts were made to restrain, or call to public service, those attempting to become monks; and severe penalties were established against anyone trying to avoid either military or fiscal obligations.

In justifying his exercise of supreme imperial power, Valentinian asserted his prerogative as lord of this world (Amm. 39.5,46) that gave him absolute right to pursue the secular well-being of the empire. In so doing he had purposefully recalled the titles used by the pre-christian roman rulers, and set about founding a dynasty by elevating his brother Valens and his own two sons to the purple. He likewise returned to the principles of roman justice, and manifested a merely superficial christian influence in his laws. He established a *defensor civitatis*—defender of the citizens—to look after the rights of individuals, an office to be assumed by the bishops in the following century, and that seems to be coming into prominence in contemporary times. Finally, he renewed the function of the corporation wherein the members of a class or public service were mutually responsible for all its obligations, from paying taxes and supplying military effectives to transport, roads, administrative and other civic necessities.

Gradually it became necessary for the government to interfere with property rights and to control or re-establish public activities down to education and to the custody of civic customs, including dress. The public educational system included the organization of universities, control of the professorships, and the conduct of the students who were allowed to pursue learning at public expense until the age of twenty, but who were also subject to public flogging and dismissal for delinquency.

In criticizing the bureaucracy and socialism of his age, and particularly the callous pleasure-seeking of the aristocratic classes, and the depredations of the lawyers, Ammianus had returned to the older standards of the stoics, and to the classic explanations for the decline of the state and public morals that destroyed "the almost incredible combination of *virtue and fortune*" which had produced the greatness of the original roman empire. He had no solution but the abolition of vice, and this the government was powerless to do, even though united by a religious force, as Valentinian's heroic but neutral efforts demonstrated.

On the death of Valentinian, Gratian had been advanced to share the emperorship with Valens, taking charge of the west. But the alliance was short-lived, for Valens died in the fatal battle of Adrianopolis (Aug. 9, 378) and, after a year of chaos in the balkan peninsula, Theodosius I was selected by the youthful emperor as his associate.

With the accession of the emperor Theodosius I (379-395), a soldier from the west and a catholic took in hand both the restoration of order in the empire itself, and the protection of its frontiers. But Theodosius attempted much more. Whereas Constantine had been content to support the outward panoply of christianity, the new emperor intended to make it the vital force in his empire. Supported by a firm belief in the trinitarian underpinning of the new religion, he attempted to use christianity as a cohesive principle to shut out subversive elements such as jews, pagans, and heretics. In so doing, he ran into the danger of exploiting the spiritual power to create a *pax terrena*, as Cochrane points out; and it was too late, for the disruptive elements in economic and social degeneration were far too advanced. While the empire took on the lineaments of catholicism, its enemies from within made peace with the barbarians on its borders, and the arian creed in a diluted form was spread among the goths, particularly by the bishop Ulfilas, to prevent their peaceful settlement for another century or more.

Meanwhile, another force that had proved disturbing during the course of the fourth century likewise took on great political significance. This was the phenomenon of monasticism. For thousands upon thousands of citizens, fleeing the rigors of the state's excessive economic burdens, turned to the law of Christ. They repudiated the claims of society and family by literally interpreting Christ's words "Go sell what you have and give it to the poor ..." They betook themselves to the open road, or the desert, determined to renounce the world utterly and finally. Their interests were turned to battling the principalities and powers of another world, that has been so vividly exemplified in the *Life of St. Anthony*. By *ascesis* and complete self-abnegation, they were preparing themselves for a new stage of existence, entirely oblivious of the empire and its immediate destiny.

This attitude had naturally infuriated Julian the Apostate; nor was it looked upon with favor by Valentinian I or the other emperors. Many of the churchmen like Jerome likewise had at least doubts as to the final intention of these recluses, particularly when, as in Syria and Egypt, they tended to form in bands and entered the streets of the great cities to enforce the power of the bishop or agitate for orthodoxy.

Nevertheless, the movement soon found its own inner direction in the guidance of men such as Pachomius in Egypt and Basil in Cappadocia, who brought order into both the daily activities and the spiritual significance of this life of seclusion. Accordingly, a sort of supernatural democracy eventuated in which prayer and the sacraments were made the basis of a communal life, one of whose requirements was hard labor and economic self-sufficiency that helped develop agriculture, the arts, crafts, and the study of christian literature, as well as, in time, the care of the sick and the poor. This movement survived the fall of the empire in the west, and became a stabilizing if not infrequently disturbing element in the emerging byzantine empire of the east. In its own form, in the west particularly under the guidance of Benedict and Gregory the Great, it was to provide the missionaries and teachers who would subdue the barbarian peoples and create the civilization of the middle ages.

Theodosius had brought order to the frontiers of the empire by making peace with the goths, and employing them to restrain the lombards and the franks. He likewise arranged a cessation of hostilities with Persia. Thus he could turn to the internal problems of his reign. He restrained the usurper Maximus at first by associating his own son Arcadius in the emperorship (383); then he eliminated Maximus in 388 when the latter attempted to overthrow Valentinian II. Upon the murder of the latter by the augenians, Theodosius put an end to the machinations of the *magister militum*, Abrogast, by investing his other son Honorius I with sovereignty in the west.

Under the pressure of the bureaucratic control of the empire, Theodosius gradually accepted the concept of a sacred monarchy. The imperial titles were invested with religious notes; the ruler became the *princeps sacratissimus*—the most sacred prince. His dwelling became the *palatium sacrum*—the sacred palace; and the ordinary citizen who had no possibility of approaching the sovereign was constrained to perform the *proskynesis* or prostration before the emperor's portrait. Gradually too, in the implementation of imperial laws, the idea of sacrilege was introduced for their infraction, bringing severe and barbarous penalties. And the custom was adopted of referring to the emperor's predecessor as "of sacred memory."

Augustine was to speak of "the faith and piety of the august Theodosius" (*Civ. Dei* 5.26), and would refer particularly to the christianization of legislation during his regime, in which the constantinian laws regarding the elimination of criminal trials during lent, and the pardon of the imprisoned, were connected with the celebration of man's redemption in the great christian feast of Easter. Likewise the old severe control of the family by the father was relaxed, and provision for the rights of mothers and children against his family were introduced.

Theodosius had begun his reign in 380 by proclaiming the catholic faith as the religion of the empire (*Cod. Theod.* 16.1.2). He then set about the extirpation of pagan superstitions, and eventually proscribed the ancient pagan religion itself beginning with legislation against divinization and sacrifice in 381. He abolished the pagan calendar of feasts and games, and introduced a christian-oriented civil year that ordained a long vacation (June 24 to October 15), and proclaimed January 1, the anniversaries of Rome and Constantinople, a two-week holiday at Easter, the anniversary of the reigning emperors, and the sundays as legal holidays. In 400, Christmas and Epiphany were added to complete the cycle in a christian sense (*Cod. Theod.* 2.8.19 and 24). It was these measures more than any other that began the successful elimination of the old historic pagan ways.

To complete this religious turnover, various heresies were denounced as public crimes, and their adherents subjected to loss of property and proscription. Finally, in 393, the jewish religion was acknowledged as licit, but its practitioners were severely limited in their civic rights.

The theodosian policy was thus directed to utilizing christianity in the service of creating a new civilization; but as such it succeeded merely in causing further confusion in the relations between the church and the empire, as subsequent events would prove. Theodosius' efforts were prosecuted in the byzantine state where, in the pursuit of orthodoxy "a political religion and a religious politics," in Cochrane's phrase, perdured for a millenium, without achieving either internal peace or external safety. In the west, while he restored the integrity of the empire, it was but an ephemeral success. However, Augustine, in line with the ancient prophets of Israel, judged the result as useful in God's inscrutable providence. For the final failure of the theodosian efforts in the west opened the way to the eventual conversion of the barbarian nations. Oblivious of this apparently providential plan, however, an actor in the drama arose with Ambrose of Milan, a man who combined imperial experience with the christian faith and possessed the integrity and fearlessness of an ancient roman magistrate.

AMBROSE OF MILAN

Ambrose had been the imperial administrator of Milan and the surrounding civil diocese; he was trained in the imperial service as a roman of the romans. He became bishop of Milan by popular acclamation in 374, a year after the death of Athanasius, in the midst of arian disturbances. Despite the fact that he was merely a catechumen at the time, and had to turn to the priest Simplician for his theological formation, he quickly seized upon the fact that, structurally and in principle, the church and the empire were two distinct entities. The church was a spiritual or sacramental institution whose essential foundation was the faith; and only one specially consecrated into her mysteries could either teach or rule in the church. The empire was thus external to the mystical order, and it could at most use its judicial structure in the service of the church, either reviewing matters that the ecclesiastical courts could not resolve, or implementing their decisions in the civil forum. [2]

Thus soteriological and sacramental considerations became primary in Ambrose's political thought, for while the church is the body of Christ, and a great mystery, its subjects are also citizens of the state. Nevertheless, Ambrose persevered in his

---

[2] On St. Ambrose, see J. Palanque, *Saint Ambroise et l'Empire romain* (Paris, 1933) and the review by M. McGuire in *Cath. Hist. Rev.* (1934); F. K. Dudden, *The Life and Times of St. Ambrose* (Oxford, 1935); S. Greenslade, *op. cit.*, 53-56; 70-78. K. Morrison, *Rome and the City of God*, 20-29; 42-51; G. Figueroa, *The Church and the Synagogues in St. Ambrose* (Washington, 1949).

loyalty to the empire, convinced that the true faith would prove a source of strength to the state, and that as the church gradually conquered paganism, the christian empire would overcome the barbarians. He differed, however, in his concepts from Eusebius, for he saw the emperor as "within the Church, not over it," and insisted that "in matters of faith, bishops are accustomed to be the judges of the christian emperors, and not emperors, of bishops" (*De fide* 2.16, 136; *Epist.* 24.4.5). [3]

In dealing with the emperor's powers and obligations, Ambrose accepted the opinion of the roman jurist, Paulus, who had declared that the emperor was above the law, since he who makes the law does not serve it. Nevertheless, Ambrose modified this interpretation in a christian sense. Commenting on the guilt that David felt at having countenanced the murder of Uriah, Ambrose says explicitly "for while the king is absolved of the law, he is still responsible to his conscience" (*In Ps.* 51.14). He thus made a distinction between the civil law as such, and the law of God. He further maintained that while God ordains all authority, he does not confer authority immediately on the user, for even the devil boasted of using power. Nor is power that is abused to be considered evil; but rather the evil is in the one who uses authority badly. For in the end it is not authority that is evil, but ambition; and he is the minister of God for good who properly exercises power (*Expos. in Lc.* 4.24).

However, Ambrose quickly saw the need for modifying the extent of the emperor's legal powers. According to Ulpian's comment on the *lex regia* or imperial power, the *jus publicum* of the ruler "extended to whatever constituted the *statum rei romanæ*"—the roman state—and this included "sacred things, priests, and magistrates" (*Instit.* 1,2). In the pagan context, Ambrose agreed; but in a christian polity—and he had the action of Gratian who had abolished the title and office of *pontifex maximus* as precedent—the *res sacræ* or sacred things of

---

[3] The use of this phrase *imperator intra ecclesiam, non supra ecclesiam est* as a principle of ecclesiastical independence has been challenged by K. Morrison who maintains (*op. cit.*, 42) that it was spoken to the catechumen Valentinian II. His observation does not seem valid.

the church were the immediate possession of God and came under the administration of the bishop. Hence in 384, when the dowager Justina had her son Valentinian II demand two basilicas of Ambrose for the use of the arians, the catholic bishop refused outright. When he was summoned before an imperial consistory to give an account of his action, he appeared with such a large group of partisans that he was allowed to depart without a hearing. In a letter (*Epist.* 21.8) he defended his action on two scores: bishops are to be tried by bishops only; and no one can command a bishop to "hand over the altars of God" (*Epist.* 20.16).

On the other hand, he was perfectly willing to admit that "the church possesses nothing except the faith" (*Epist.* 18.16) and to insist that ecclesiastics should not accept favors from the government: "The church is not a beggar!"

His point was that both the church by participation, and the altar that it protected as the body of Christ, could not belong to Caesar, since Christ excluded what belongs to God from the emperor's competence (*Serm. contra dux,* 31,35).

On the other hand, in dealing with Symmachus and the Altar of Victory removed from the senate house, Ambrose insisted that "everyone had the right to freely defend and preserve the faith and purpose of his own mind" (*Epist.* 17.7). Thus he vindicated the right of christian senators not to be forced to carry on their affairs under the patronage of a pagan god. He maintained that the abolishment of the privileges and state support for the pagan priesthood and its temples was just and proper, since it was a step in the direction of full freedom for all religious practice. But when Symmachus maintained that equal rights should be granted to both the pagan and the christian religions, appurtenances and practices, Ambrose demurred on the score that paganism was obviously a false religion.

Actually, however, while he quoted the principle that equity confirms the commands [of emperors] and injustice dissolves them (*De off.* 2.19), he had in mind the law of the faith as establishing final equity. In this he is not unlike a roman praetor in the days of the republic established to provide justice; but the justice provided was what was equitable in the mind of the law-enforcing magistrate.

In the end Ambrose vindicated the right of the christian to freedom, and would afford tolerance to jews and pagans as long as they conformed to the laws of the empire. His clash with Theodosius over the punishment of christians for the burning of the jewish synagogue at Callinicum in 388, and his threat of excommunication of the emperor after the massacre at Thessalonica, were instances of his interference with matters of public order that he maintained had become a *"causa Dei"* and therefore required the active interest of the bishop.

The authority exercised by Ambrose had a far-reaching influence on the development of political thought in the west, and while it strengthened the alliance between the church and the empire, it indicated the independence that should be the bishop's prerogative—a quality to be contested frequently, all during the next millenium. Ambrose's concept of civil responsibility, along with the ideal of the supremacy of the spiritual, was a large factor in preventing the church from being involved in the disaster that befell the western empire with its final overthrow by the barbarians.

While all the catholic churchmen at least were perfectly willing to admit with Paul, and the traditional teaching, that the emperor's authority came from God, there were limits to the regal power, as the catholic bishops had maintained all through the constantinian period. One of those limits was reached in the juridical murder of Priscillian, the spanish leader of an ascetical movement that had been condemned in a synod at Saragossa in 380 A.D. There is some confusion regarding the details of the case as reported by Sulpitius Severus in his *Chronicon* (2.47), and by Priscillian himself in his Letter to Pope Damasus (*Tract.* 11). But after the consecration of Priscillian as bishop of Avila by his two episcopal supporters, Instantius and Salvian, an appeal to Rome was made in person by the three bishops against the charge of heresy. When they were rebuffed by both the bishop of Rome, and by Ambrose of Milan, they had recourse to the emperor, and received a rescript restoring them to their episcopal sees.

Upon the assassination of the emperor Gratian in 383, however, the usurper Maximus was anxious to display his complete orthodoxy, and Priscillian and Instantius were brought to Bordeaux for a synodal trial in 384. Priscillian appealed once more to the emperor, and was brought to Trier. There he was charged with witchcraft *(maleficia)* and imprisoned, despite the protest of Martin of Tours. Tried by the prefect Evodius, he was sentenced to death with six companions, and the emperor gave his consent. The event caused great difficulty to a number of bishops and pope Siricius, bishop Ambrose of Milan, and Martin of Tours refused communion with the bishops who had consented to the trial and execution. While this event stirred the consciences of the western churchmen, a similar but much more extensive problem concerning the relations of the emperor and the church was troubling the christian life of North Africa.

THE DONATISTS

The problem posed by the donatists in North Africa had served as an unregistered warning that the constantinian concept of the emperor as supreme lord in both church and state was unworkable in the christian dispensation. The movement was a result of a dispute concerning the position in the church of those who had lapsed into apostasy or compromised their faith during the persecutions.

The catholic bishops for the most part proved lenient in their judgment of these poor renegades. The donatists reacted against them with vigor; then drew conclusions concerning the worthiness of the minister of the sacraments that made his spiritual effectiveness depend upon his own spiritual qualities and sentiments. This stand was considered an unwarranted interference with God's ability to confer grace through the sacramental actions, despite the possible unworthiness of the minister, and in accordance with the good faith of the recipient. From a dispute, the situation worsened into schism; and upon the emancipation of the church, the donatist bishops in Africa demanded recognition of the emperor by the restoration of their property. Constantine, as we have seen, submitted their case to several western synods at their request; when the judgment went against them, he tried physical force; then, finding this useless, he left them to their own deserts. [4]

The local governors in North Africa, however, were continually faced with rebellion and turbulence, for as the movement grew it was proclaimed a more or less national expression of true christianity. It became a martyr church and underwent a millenarist revolution so that Tyconius could represent the resistance of the donatists to both catholic persuasion and governmental pressure as the first act in the final struggle between the forces of evil and the kingdom of God:

> "As has been done in Africa,"
> he wrote, "so it will happen
> in the whole world. Then
> the Antichrist will be revealed
> as he has been partly among us.
> Through Africa, the whole church
> will become manifest" *(Comm. on apoc. of Beatus).*

In consequence of this belief, bands of devotees and monks from the poorer classes roamed the countryside and to the cry of *deo laudes*, forced landlords to free their slaves and indemnify their debtors. When they met a rich man being driven in his carriage, they forced him to change places with his footman with the words of the magnificat—*deposuit potentes de sede, et exaltavit humiles:* "he put the powerful down from their seat and exalted the humble." By thus insisting upon the apocalyptic and other worldly aspects of the christian creed, these schismatics destroyed public order and engendered the fanaticism to be met with all through the history of the church on the part of what K. Holl and Ronald Knox have described as "enthusiasm." [5]

---

[4] P. Monceaux, *Histoire littéraire de l'Afrique Chrétienne* (Paris, 1912-1922), 4-6; W. Frend, *The Donatist Church* (Oxford, 1952); C. Dawson, *Dynamics of World History* (New York, 1956), 298-300.

[5] See K. Holl, *Enthusiasmus und Bussgewalt* (Leipzig, 1898); R. Knox, *Enthusiasm* (New York, 1950), 50-70.

This problem bothered succeeding reigns of the emperors who tried every conceivable means of dealing with it. In his first approaches, Augustine deplored the use of force on the part of the government; but when he and his community were victimized he began to change his attitude. In any case, a large part of his time as a priest and bishop was spent in synods and discussions with the donatists; and through his basically pacific overtures, the back of the movement was broken. But the phenomenon entered into his final estimate of the problem presented by the political order and the city of God.

Meanwhile, Jerome had expressed some concern about the reason for Paul's admonition regarding the necessity for subjection to the power of the civil ruler, as he quoted the caution to Titus: "Admonish them to be subject to princes and powers" (Tit 3,1). He seemed to think it was against a spirit of libertinism encouraged by the disciples of Judas Galileus in the primitive church. On the words of Christ concerning the tribute to Caesar, he believed that Paul in Romans was commenting on that matthean pericope, and explained that in the greek text Paul emphasized "principalities more than the princes and powers of this world." Paul, he said, referred to the power, not to the men wielding it. Hence if what the prince commands is legitimate, it is to be obeyed. If not, "and it seems against God," Peter's caution: "We must obey God rather than men" is to be followed (*Comment. in Tit.* 3). [6]

In his Commentary on Daniel, Jerome was concerned much more with refuting the assertions of the anti-christian polemicist, Porphyry, who claimed—justifiably as modern exegesis has ascertained—that the prophetic parts of the book of Daniel were written after the fact instead of before. In the end Jerome concluded that even should Porphyry be correct, there was no great harm done to christian teaching.

On the political pattern behind history, he predicated a close connection between divine providence and the unfolding of human events. While he elaborated on the rise and fall of

---

[6] On Jerome, see F. X. Murphy, *A Monument to St. Jerome* (New York, 1952), 114-141; O. Antin, *Essai sur S. Jérome* (Paris, 1951).

the four kingdoms, there is not a deterministic or apocalyptic turn to his theory. He maintained, and he might be quoting Hesiod or Solon rather than Isaiah or Daniel, that the corruption and downfall of these great states had been due to pride and rapacity on the part of their rulers and people. Hence he was not surprised to see signs of disaster piling up against the roman empire of his own times (*Com. in Dan.* 3.40).

There is some question as to Jerome's having been influenced by the anti-empirical literature of the augustan age, as he seems to show a special familiarity with the Philippic History of Pompeius Trogus, and departs in his *Chronicon* from the assessment of the four kingdoms made by his model, Eusebius of Caesarea. It is highly improbable that Jerome was familiar enough with this literature to be a conscious critic of the augustan policy. His learning here was compilatory; his citations of pagan authors mainly secondhand; and his interests much more biblical than political. On the other hand, detailing the possible immediate application of the prophecy of Isaiah (chapter 60) to his own times, he commented:

> This can be taken in either a material or a spiritual sense. If in the former, we see the roman caesars bending their necks to the yoke of Christ; building churches at the public expense; and leveling the fiats of law against the persecutions of the gentiles and the attacks of heretics ... Although we now experience these things coming to pass in the church, they will be more fully carried out upon the consummation of the world in the second coming of the Savior. (*Com. in Is.* 60.10ff.).

Jerome's political perspicacity is revealed in his incidental judgments on the happenings of his age. In commenting on the writings and influence of Lactantius concerning the constantinian attempt to christianize his world, Jerome remarked: "Would that he had stated our position as effectively as he demolished that of our opponents" (*Epist.* 58.10). In reviewing the maneuvers of Julian the Apostate as he gradually eliminated christians from education and the military, Jerome says that he exercised a "mild *(blanda)* persecution, convincing rather than impelling to sacrifice" (*Transl. chron. Eus.* 2 [Ann. 366]).

He found Valentinian's law nullifying bequests by widows and orphans to their spiritual directors "deplorable, not as law, but as indicating the scandalous conditions that prompted it" (*Cod. Theod.* 16.2.20). But his true sensibilities as a roman, laying the foundations for an authentic christian scholarship in his retreat at Bethlehem, escaped him, when on hearing of the sack of Rome by Alaric in 410, he exclaimed: *Domine, venerunt gentes in hereditatem tuam,* "Lord the gentiles have overrun your inheritance"! (*Ps.* 78).

9

The Augustinian Evaluation

With Augustine, a new notion is introduced into the realm of christian political thought. He came to his conclusions about political philosophy by a great detour that began with the criteriological principle *crede ut intellegas*, believe that you may understand. But he was not advocating a mere fideism. His arsenal of philosophical criticism used against the ancient gods and contemporary moral myths was more devastating than that of all the cynics and epicureans together; but when he had torn asunder the pagan deities and the false presuppositions of secularism, he had a doctrine with which to fill the void. It was not a mere ideology, a current of thought that represented a conviction based on a new approach to logic, or physics, or psychology, or history. It was rather a theology, and it embraced all these human disciplines; but it both demonstrated their vacuity without a solid, spiritual underpinning and, by supplying that foundation, led to the total employment of those means in a conception of man. [1]

Presented with the problem of the downfall of the roman empire, symbolized in the sack of Rome itself by Alaric and the Goths in 410 A.D., Augustine was constrained by the critics

---

[1] Cf. C. Dawson, "St. Augustine and the City of God," *The Dynamics of History* (New York, 1956), 294-325; C. Cochrane, *Christianity and Classical Culture* (Oxford, 1944), 381-455; C. Combès, *La Doctrine politique de S. Augustin* (Paris, 1927).

of christianity to consider the problem of the *polis* and the hellenic *politeia*. The pagans claimed that it was the christian creed with its rejection of the gods, and its ultimate flight from the *sæculum* or world that was responsible for the destruction of the great roman civilization inaugurated in the augustan age. Instead of rushing into print to refute this charge, Augustine employed some fourteen years (412-426) in the composition of his *City of God*. Hence it is no mere monograph or compilation, but a vast synthesis of his mature response to all the problems faced by the conscientious individual who desired to know who he is, what he is doing in the world, and what can be known of his destiny.

While Augustine's knowledge of history is deficient according to modern standards, and while he writes as an african with possibly a partial territorial prejudice against Rome, he is not writing history but political science. And that science is not merely terrestrial in its boundaries, but it looks beyond the immediate rise and fall of kingdoms to contemplate their true evaluation in relation to the kingdom of God.

In this respect, he is far from an idealist, although his perspective is basically transcendent in a platonic sense. Actually, one of his objectives was to destroy the platonic dream that he eventually found to be a fundamentally evil influence in human thought, leading to dualism and a flight from the facts of life. His feet were firmly planted in the world, and his mind was focused on the human psychology of his contemporaries, both compatriots and foreigners. What he set out to prove was the simple fact that the cosmos with all its apparatus of terror and magnificence did not explain man; nor could man explain the cosmos without taking into consideration a series of happenings that had left their mark upon the course of human history in such fashion that they must be believed in order to be seen. Thus he utilized the admonition *crede ut intellegas*—believe that you may understand—as a tool for prying loose the bands that, while holding the problem of world history together, obscured its perception.

He rejected all attempts to introduce poetical myth into the explanation of man's primitive history as nothing but a phenomenon utilized by intelligent but uninformed theogonists and philosophers. He repudiated the notion of the imperial, civic, and household gods, and with them all the paraphernalia of the augurs and the soothsayers. But he likewise called into question the rational constructs of a political philosophy based on human or abstract justice with its concomitant virtues of civic service and a striving for excellence that had characterized the best efforts of the stoics and was given classic expression in Cicero.

Ambrose had rejected the ciceronian doctrine concerned with man's purpose in life that directed the citizen's talents and energies to the pursuit of virtue in the service of the community or state-*officia*. He did so, despite the fact that at first sight this doctrine seemed to be a secular reflection of the attitude of the primitive christians who, in Luke's idealized description, lived a communal life with charity one for the other. And Ambrose had justified the rejection by pointing to the fact that the ciceronian objective was the achievement of the *beata vita*, the blessed life. Its optic was too limited; it was earth-bound. For the christian, his objective was *vita eterna*, life in God both here and hereafter.

It was only this concept of man's destiny that could give substance to the idea of *philanthropia* or love for one's fellow-men. While idealistic in proposal, the stoic program concerned with fraternal charity lacked sufficient reason to make it viable. To tell a man he was part of a cosmic process and therefore should love his fellowman might have an appeal to the philosopher; but it sounded like sheer nonsense to the ordinary person who felt he had a thousand reasons for despising most of his neighbors.

But to inform a man that he should love his neighbor because he was his brother, with a personal and loving God as their common father, was a different proposition. And in the christian concept, this obligation was given a peculiarly human twist when he was told "you should love your neighbor as yourself" for the love of God.

It is this principle that Augustine seized upon as the core of his political theorizings. He demonstrated that the avarice and hatreds, the oppression and exploitation that characterized the great states of secular history, contradicted the principle of love, and brought each nation to its final destruction. Then, using charity as the talisman of mundane human relations, he showed that merely human love is impossible without a recognition of divine love that has existed in the history of the world from the moment of creation, and that precedes creation in the Trinity.   With Athanasius, he realized that only the trinitarian concept could in the end fully justify the history of man's salvation with its culmination in man's redemption by the passion, death, and resurrection of Christ.

As for the political virtues of prudence or wisdom, justice, fortitude, and temperance, they only came fully to term if they were enlightened by grace. But the enlightenment of grace is not an illumination from without; it is rather a god-given endowment that pervades the totality of a man's being and begins with faith. Thus the christian, once determined upon turning from evil to goodness, overcomes one of the primary obstacles to wisdom among the greeks, *hubris* or arrogance. For it is only with a truly humble heart that he can accept the evidence of faith.   Thereafter, likewise, the requirement of contrition and penance to which he is enabled by grace as part of his conversion, is a salutary lesson in total self-honesty, and the ability to judge what goes on outside himself with a critical if benevolent eye.

Augustine saw both the exemplar and the safeguards for this way of life built into the church, which is the mystical body of Christ. And while the church has a para-political structure, using some of the methods of secular government in its activities in the world, it is actually in its sacramental system that it gives meaning and substance to the governance and grace-giving activities of the hierarchy and priesthood. Finally, while he respected the need for civil government, he rejected the idea that any state could represent the kingdom of God. Even the visible church, though the body of Christ, is not quite equivalent to the city of God, since its membership is wider than that of the actual believers at any moment in history. It reaches from creation to the second coming of Christ, and it contains all mankind who avail themselves of the redemption they have been given in Christ's death and resurrection.

Augustine's perspective was narrowed apparently by his own experience with sin, both personal and that of his contemporaries, as well as through his reading of history. Hence he tends to be a pessimist as to the number of those who are actually saved. And with rigorous logic he finds no difficulty in excusing God's justice in damning limitless numbers of human beings—the *massa damnata*. But this ruthlessness is a personal conviction and does not affect his political theorizing in substance, though it does make him a harsher judge of human failure than the general run of christians.

Thanks to his preoccupation with the concept of time, and the breakthrough he accomplished by recognizing the fact that the human race had had an absolute beginning, and was headed in a straight line for just as absolute an ending, he "exploded the perpetual cycles" of hellenic thought. Thus he broke with platonism, as he saw that time was not a perpetually revolving maze of eternity; but rather a unique consciousness of before, present, and future, making man's destiny an irreversible process moving in a definite direction. Christ is this straight way, as he is its life and truth; hence in Christ is the guarantee of man's free will and of his redemption from the fate of cyclic recurrence, as well as from sin.

Augustine discovered that the nature of time was essentially connected with created beings as a whole, and not merely with the movement of the heavenly bodies. What is more, it was the function of a living intelligence to be conscious of the present moment, able to recall past things that had receded into nothingness, and looking forward to the future: *mane quippe in eis factum est et vespere:* things have a dawning, then pass away in their own twilight (*Conf.* 13.35). That future that does not now exist is not far away; but only as one's expectation of it is more or less protracted, does it seem to be greatly distant.

The significance of this realization on Augustine's part is the fact that it brought him to a new idea as to the nature of history. Since man is the recorder of time, then the recognition of his existence and his experiences proceeds in a progressive line. It is not a continuous and meaningless repetition. The past is incorporated in the experience of humanity; and man is capable of making progress in culture and spiritual growth for his own satisfaction and for the well-being of society.

Questions have been raised as to how far Augustine realized the implications of his discovery, since, in talking of the city of God, that spiritual achievement of those whose love is directed to divine things, he seemed to overstress an eternal and predestined order. But there is his knowledge of Christ's parables that he continually comments upon in his sermons to show his awareness of "the bad and the good seed growing together until the harvest," and in the end his description of world history comes down to that simple fact.

"Two loves built two cities" is his thesis; and he saw the two cities—the *politeuma* of those who love God and obey his commands; and the *politeia* of those who love themselves and fall into the snares of the demons:

> running their course together, intermingling one with another all through the changes of time from the beginning of the human race. They shall continue to develop together until the end of the world, when they are to be separated at the last judgment. (*De civ. Dei* 14.1,28).

In books 15 to 18 of his *City of God*, Augustine attempted to demonstrate this occurrence by a brief review of world history seen in this perspective. He described the worldly city as the mystical Babylon, and found its two most important manifestations in the empires of Assyria and Rome, to which as he says "all other kingdoms are but appendages." He paralleled this wave of secular history with the development of the heavenly city from its inception with the patriarchs, through the history of Israel, and the holy city of Jerusalem, to its final concretization in the christian experience and the catholic church.

In viewing these historical phenomena, he uses as his value yardstick the principle *non faciunt bonos vel malos mores, nisi boni vel mali amores :* it is only good or evil loves that make good or evil morals. Hence at first sight he seems to agree with Tertullian and Commodian who disavowed the secular civilization, and saw in the state merely the glorification of human pride and selfishness, stimulated by the demons. In this sense, Augustine does seem to justify his concept of man as vitiated by concupiscence from the start by the original sin of the first man. The human race is a *massa damnata* that has been spared perdition through the condescension of the son of God. But the redemption meant more than a mere relief from the bonds of Satan. It signified a total reconditioning of man's make-up as a "new creature" such as it is preached by St. Paul.

With Cyprian, Augustine felt that the kingdoms of the world were founded on injustice, and that they progressed through exploitation, bloodshed, and war. This was particularly true of Rome, in which he had felt the terrible weight of human suffering that its rise and accomplishment represented:

> "The imperial city," he wrote, "endeavors to communicate her language to all the lands she has subdued. She then desires to procure a fuller society and a greater abundance of interpreters on both sides. But how many lives has this cost? And suppose that it is accomplished, the worst is not past for ... wider extension of her empires will produce still greater wars.... Whoever considers these extremes of sorrow and bloodshed with compassion must concede that all this is a mystery. He who contemplates them without a sorrowful reaction or even some comprehension is far more wretched than he realizes. For he imagines he has achieved the bliss of a god, when he has deprived himself of the natural feelings of a man" (*De civ. Dei* 19.7).

Augustine eventually found himself forced to reject the opinion of Cicero, who maintained that essentially the foundations of the state rested on justice. Citing the innumerable injustices committed by the roman praetors and magistrates in the name of righteousness, describing the torture of innocent witnesses, and the judicial murder of guiltless victims of unreasonable laws, he decided that if justice were the criterion for the establishment of a state, the roman empire itself could not be considered a state. On the other hand, the only organized society in which justice truly ruled was the city of God. But this was obviously not a state in the political sense. Hence, he concluded that every human society found its constituent principle in a common will. He thus defined a nation or people as a "multitude of rational creatures associated in a common agreement, working toward the things it loves" (*De civ. Dei* 19.24). He avoided all reference to moral elements in his definition of the state, and described it merely as motivated toward a common objective, no matter whether that should be good or bad.

As C. Dawson observed, this apparent moral callousness shocked many of Augustine's nineteenth century commentators, such as A. J. Carlyle. But it fits in with the realism of twentieth century political concepts, just as it reflects the tactical discussion of statism on the part of a Thucydides among the ancients, or a Machiavelli in the renaissance. It is a recognition of a fact; hence it need not be judged either cynical or amoral. But as a political recognition it should help the right-minded man and particularly the christian to direct his loyalties to their proper ends. Thus Augustine frequently insisted that christianity made good citizens, and that the true remedy for the ills of society was to be found in the same power that heals the moral weakness of the individual soul.

Thus he maintained:

> Here also is security for the welfare and renown of the republic. For no state is perfectly established and preserved if not on the foundations and by the bond of firm faith and concord. This can only come about when the highest and truest good, namely, God, is loved by all, and men loving each other in him without discrimination, because they love one another for his sake. (*Epist.* 137.18; 138.15-17).

Epilogue

In this brief survey of political thought covering over a thousand years of human experience, much has been omitted through design as well as by inadvertence. Almost no attention has been given to a host of pagan political philosophers from Theocritus and Polybius to Seneca and Marcus Aurelius, and little notice has been taken of the papacy. In the first case, the plethora of writers made it necessary to select and choose; but it is felt that the main ideas of the pre-christian political thought were at least touched upon. In the matter of the papacy, other than as bishops, the popes made practically no pronouncements and played no recognizable part in the political sphere down to the times of Leo I (440-461); and his activities go beyond the period of our immediate interest. Almost nothing is said, likewise, of the economic and social conditions that affected the political development all during this period; but this is due to the failure of the age itself to take other than a cursory interest in these important matters.

The four hundred years of the christian experiment in dealing with the political organization of human life indicate clearly that in the civil sphere, at least, christianity was not intended as a directly revolutionary force. The kingdom of God toward whose achievement the life of the christian is aimed has no true habitat or institutional existence in this world. Nor has the christian had much greater success in injecting justice and right reason into the conduct of political affairs than the people of previous or other religious or secular dispensations.

What seems clear from this brief and simplified account of the history of political thought and action between Homer and Augustine is the fact that in almost every age there were men dedicated to teaching the ideals of justice and philanthropy or charity. Hesiod and Solon, as well as Hippolytus and Augustine, spoke of the just and the unjust *polis*—of the city of God and the city of the evil demon. What Augustine did was present a panorama of man's political experiences, judging the accomplishments and failures by the norms of the love of God and of one's fellowmen. On this score, he was not too far removed from the more serious of the political philosophers who preceded him. Nor were the christian churchmen who insisted on man's right to worship God, and to pursue the currents of political life in freedom and security, greatly different from their pagan predecessors, although they dealt with diverse situations.

What is involved essentially in the christian attitude toward politics is a commitment to the things of this world on the part of one who recognizes the present creation as instinct with mystery—the mystery of man's impermanence on this globe and his insatiable seeking after justice. The latter is an innate desire, while the former is a fact; and these two conditions of human experience seem to be connected both with man's destiny and with his propensity to act against the dictates of right reason.

What seems difficult to explain is the fact that in both the experience of the pagan whose religious thinking was not buttressed by a direct divine revelation, and in the judeo-christian experience where this overreaching element is present, there does not seem to be a substantial difference in the matter of achieving terrestrial justice. Nor on a more pedestrian plane is there much evidence of greater, sustained practice of brotherly love among christians than there is among the pagans. For the latter in all civilizations had at least analogous concepts and practices of philanthropy. Here and there in the judeo-christian experience there have been exceptional and outstanding examples of the heroic practice of fraternal charity, but the judgment of G. K. Chesterton, despite an obvious exaggeration, still has a ring of reality: "Christianity has not been tried and found wanting. It has been found difficult and not tried."

The problem that thus presents itself is simply the question of how far is the christian committed to concerning himself with the temporal order? Since the freedom granted to the church with the conversion of Constantine, there is no question but that christians generally, and the church as a temporal organization, have devoted tremendous effort to the problem of politics. Throughout the middle ages in the west at least, and all during the byzantine experience, the church was intimately involved in the political order. Yet there were men in the church who singly and in groups maintained that this was not the church's business. In recent times, in particular, the church has gradually drawn back from immediate involvement. But this is due as much to the historical circumstances of the age as it is to principle or conviction.

During the age of exclusion, the apologists and early church fathers had no idea of immixing spiritual and political matters. This is obvious from the history here narrated. After the first enthusiastic reaction of a Lactantius and a Eusebius, the majority of christian writers and thinkers returned to the pauline doctrine that required obedience to the civil authorities but made no provision for the christian to enter into the political arena. They interpreted Christ's comment, "Render unto Caesar the things that are Caesar's" in a sense that seemed to exclude the christian *politeia* from a direct involvement in the secular *polis*. And when the emperor became christian, and set about converting the system of government to conformity with christian ideals, it was quickly realized that legislating holiness was an impossibility. This is the final conclusion of Augustine; and after a thousand years of experimentation with every conceivable type of political involvement from the caesaro-papism of the byzantine polity to the medieval and modern experience of the papal states, the judgment is sustained.

The contemporary christian thus finds himself with little hope of obtaining direction from history as he approaches the problem of religion and the modern state. Nor is there much immediate encouragement for him in the recent pronounce- ment of the Pastoral Constitution on the Church in the Contemporary World that explicitly deals with man's political commitment (part II, chap. 5).

For the conciliar fathers quickly realized that the church does not have a political doctrine in the sense of an ideal set of principles or laws for the governance of a particular nation or state. It has principles with regard to justice and charity that lead to the practice of political virtues within the state. It has cautions and admonitions against evildoing in the political order; and consolation and encouragement for men oppressed by totalitarian despotisms. But it possesses no true theology of politics.

In a less sophisticated age, the "principalities and powers, and dominations" guiding if not ruling the destinies of nations were interpreted as angels and demons in an anthropomorphic throwback. This approach is hardly acceptable today. Yet every age has it own demons. For there are forces and elements in the behavior of nations and peoples, as there are in the conduct of individuals, that reveal themselves as inimical to the requirements of justice and decency in the pursuit of the political destiny of a nation, just as sin and perversion haunt the conduct of the individual in the pursuit of goodness and happiness. It is here that mystery enters the scene on both the cosmic and the individual level. And it is here that christianity presents an explanation of man's plight both as a person and as part of a nation and a people.

With christianity there enters the idea of God as a trinity, and of Christ, the son of God, incarnate in this world. Accom- panying the incarnation is the notion of original sin, and of the redemption with man's destiny in a final deification as the goal of his terrestrial experience. Where christianity does appear inadequate to the secular mind is precisely on the political level; for while proclaiming the individual as a member of the "people of God," the christian faith gives no precise or specific ordinance as to the worldly organization of that people. Without organization, the pursuit of terrestrial activity is impossible. Thus there seems to be a vacuum in the christian theology requiring recourse to philosophy; and this brings about an immediate ambivalence—for the two disciplines are neither coextensive nor fully reconcilable. The one looks to man's conduct in view of an eschatalogical destiny; the other views man as engaged in constructing an earthly *polis* ordered to justice and charity.

The solution to the dilemma thus posed would seem to lie in a pluralism that clearly distinguishes between the temporal order and that of religion. This is not to be taken in the sense that politics has an end contrary to religion. Rather it means that politics is concerned with the ordering of the secular city in the pursuit of justice; but that human experience thus far indicates that justice is impossible unless the men dedicated to its pursuit are motivated by higher ideals. In the search for such ideals, man must take into consideration his final destiny that is beyond politics. To this extent, then, religion will have a bearing on politics in that it serves as a guideline and aid in securing the substantiality of justice to which the political order is directed; it should likewise obtain the adhesion of religious minded men in furthering the ends of the *polis* while they are engaged in the pilgrimage stage of their existence journeying toward eternity and union with God.

The sum total of human experience thus far testifies to the fact that with Virgil *sunt lacrimæ rerum*—there are tears in things. But there are also with Wordsworth "intimations of immortality" in human affairs. And behind man's activities and consciousness, there is at least a suggestion of a divinity. Politics, the most worldly of human endeavors, is instinct with theological preoccupations and motives. To attempt to wash out the lineaments of a divine providence in human affairs because of the horrible crimes and the superstitions committed in the name of a god or in the pursuit of a true religion is simply to mismanage the evidence. The best a man can do, therefore, is with Athanasius and Augustine to come to terms with the evidence and to pursue the traces of divinity in human affairs.

What seems obvious is the necessity of acknowledging a trinity in the godhead, for such an idea adds a dimension to man's consciousness and essential dignity that justifies the only relationship that can bring peace and tranquility in men's relations with one another. Love of one's neighbor is simply a ridiculous idea if man is not his brother's keeper. It is this idea that is missing from the ancient hellenic experience for the most part, although it was preached by the stoics. But in their philosophy it was based upon a pantheistic notion that had little personal meaning to the individual. In the christian dispensation, on the other hand, man is his brother's keeper, because all are one with Christ, the son of God.

While great things were accomplished along the line of a true and generous philanthropy by men in ancient civilizations, and while much was left undone along this very line by christian men and believers all down the course of history, this need not be an indication that either the religious foundation does not exist, or that man in his human condition is incapable of rising to the height of divine expectation. The christian creed calls for a conversion of the individual, a dying of the old man, and a rising with Christ to a new life. Should a majority of mankind take this requirement seriously, there is bound to be a revolution in the political order. The modern experience of revolutions in science, in industry, in the tremendous effort being made to help underdeveloped peoples help themselves, indicates that nothing is impossible to man once he makes up his mind to strive for a new ordering of worldly affairs. Why cannot such a revolution be sought in the political order, based upon a revolutionary adherence to the christian religion? This was what Christ called for in praying to his Father, "that they all may be one in me, as I am in thee." It was the vision of the terrestrial *politeia* indulged in by pope John XXIII when he wrote his magnificent encyclical *Pacem in terris*—Peace on Earth.

INDEX

Imprimi potest :
G. De Ceuninck, C.SS.R., Vicarius Generalis,
Rome, September 17, 1967.

Imprimatur :
Tornaci, die 20 octobris 1967.
J. Thomas, vic. gen.